# 100

## THINGS TO DO IN

# SYRACUSE

## BEFORE YOU

# DIE

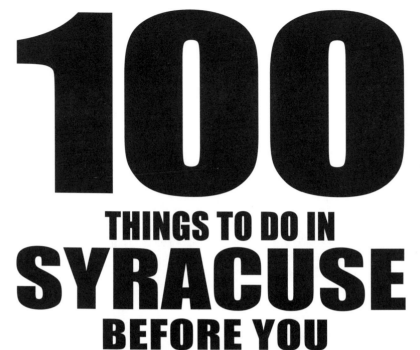

# 100
## THINGS TO DO IN
# SYRACUSE
## BEFORE YOU
# DIE

## LINDA LOWEN

REEDY PRESS

Library of Congress Control Number: 2021950837

ISBN: 9781681063522

Design by Jill Halpin

Interior photos by Sandy Roe.
Cover photo by Dongmin Shin.

Printed in the United States of America
22 23 24 25 26  5 4 3 2 1

# DEDICATION

For Mr. Green, who shows me every day
why happily-ever-after isn't Hawaii . . .
and for Jaye the adventurer and Em the homeowner,
together my proudest achievements.

# CONTENTS

**Acknowledgments**. . . . . . . . . . . . . . . . . . . . . . . . . . . . . . . . . . . . . . . . . . xii

**Preface**. . . . . . . . . . . . . . . . . . . . . . . . . . . . . . . . . . . . . . . . . . . . . . . . xiv

**Food and Drink**

   **1.** Anticipate While You Wait at Dinosaur Bar-B-Que . . . . . . . . . . . . 2

   **2.** Savor Global Goodies at Salt City Market. . . . . . . . . . . . . . . . . . . 3

   **3.** Fall for Hot Tom at Pastabilities . . . . . . . . . . . . . . . . . . . . . . . . . . 4

   **4.** Crown the Champ of Chicken Riggies. . . . . . . . . . . . . . . . . . . . . . . 5

   **5.** Cuisine-Hop in Armory Square . . . . . . . . . . . . . . . . . . . . . . . . . . . 6

   **6.** Toast the Knights of Ni at Middle Ages Brewing . . . . . . . . . . . . . . 8

   **7.** Breakfast 'til You Burst at Mother's Cupboard . . . . . . . . . . . . . . . . 9

   **8.** Trade Blarney at Coleman's Authentic Irish Pub . . . . . . . . . . . . . . 10

   **9.** Stuff Yourself Silly at the New York State Fair. . . . . . . . . . . . . . . . 11

  **10.** Caffeinate and Cowork at Café Kubal . . . . . . . . . . . . . . . . . . . . . . 12

  **11.** Circle Hanover Square for Breakfast, Lunch, and Dinner . . . . . . . . 14

  **12.** Pick Apples and More at Beak & Skiff and 1911 Established. . . . . 15

  **13.** Decide the Diner Throw-Down over the Fretta . . . . . . . . . . . . . . . . 16

  **14.** Surrender to Flavor at the Cider Mill. . . . . . . . . . . . . . . . . . . . . . . 17

  **15.** Holler at What a Dollar Gets You at Taste of Syracuse. . . . . . . . . . 18

  **16.** *Mangia* Old World Specialties in Little Italy. . . . . . . . . . . . . . . . . 20

  **17.** Risk Brain Freeze at Gannon's Ice Cream. . . . . . . . . . . . . . . . . . . . 22

  **18.** Dine Inn Style at a Cazenovia Landmark . . . . . . . . . . . . . . . . . . . . 23

• • • • • • • • • • • • • • • • • • • • • • • • • • • •

**19.** Polish Off a Polish Feast at Eva's. . . . . . . . . . . . . . . . . . . . . . . 24

**20.** Wolf a Dog or Coney at Heid's . . . . . . . . . . . . . . . . . . . . . . 25

**21.** Raise a Glass to Freedom at Luna Loca. . . . . . . . . . . . . . . . . 26

**22.** Head to the Hills for Microbrews and Views. . . . . . . . . . . . . 27

## Music and Entertainment

**23.** Be One in a Million at the Great New York State Fair . . . . . . . . . 30

**24.** Revel in the Dazzle of the Landmark Theatre . . . . . . . . . . . . . . 31

**25.** Keep the Doctor Away at the Lafayette Apple Festival . . . . . . . . 32

**26.** Baum around Oz-Stravaganza and All Things Oz . . . . . . . . . . . . 33

**27.** Immerse Yourself in the Otherworldly Museum of Intrigue . . . . . . 34

**28.** Triple Your Fun at the Oncenter . . . . . . . . . . . . . . . . . . . . . . . 36

**29.** Choose Your Musical Groove at a Symphoria Concert. . . . . . . . . 37

**30.** Dance to Live Music in an Orchard at Beak & Skiff . . . . . . . . . . . 38

**31.** Add Drama to Your Life at Syracuse Stage . . . . . . . . . . . . . . . . . 39

**32.** Strut Your Stuff at the NYS Blues Festival . . . . . . . . . . . . . . . . . 40

**33.** Fly High at the Jamesville Balloonfest . . . . . . . . . . . . . . . . . . . . 41

**34.** Pump Up the Volume at St. Joe's Amp . . . . . . . . . . . . . . . . . . . . 42

**35.** Eat, Drink, and Chill at Winterfest . . . . . . . . . . . . . . . . . . . . . . 43

**36.** Consider Yourself Irish on Green Beer Sunday. . . . . . . . . . . . . . 44

**37.** Applaud the Arts Warmly at Redhouse . . . . . . . . . . . . . . . . . . . . 46

**38.** Feel *Wilkommen* at Inclusive Wunderbar. . . . . . . . . . . . . . . . . . 47

**39.** Keep It Reel at the Syracuse International Film Festival. . . . . . . . 48

**40.** Harvest Happy Memories at Critz Farms . . . . . . . . . . . . . . . . . . 49

**41.** Jam at These Jumpin' Joints for Live Music . . . . . . . . . . . . . . . . 50

● ● ● ● ● ● ● ● ● ● ● ● ● ● ● ● ● ● ● ● ● ● ● ● ●

## Sports and Recreation

**42.** Follow Where Mules Once Trod along the Erie Canal . . . . . . . . . . 54

**43.** Drop "Carrier" and Just Call It The Dome . . . . . . . . . . . . . . . . . 56

**44.** Walk on (What Once Was) Water at Clinton Square . . . . . . . . . . . 57

**45.** Stroll Onondaga Lake Park, the "Central Park of CNY" . . . . . . . . 58

**46.** Swear You're in the Caribbean at Green Lakes . . . . . . . . . . . . . . 60

**47.** Play All Day at the Entertainment Venues of Destiny USA . . . . . . 61

**48.** Flock to the Mall to View Bald Eagles . . . . . . . . . . . . . . . . . . . . 62

**49.** Get Lit on a Cold Winter's Night at Lights on the Lake . . . . . . . . 63

**50.** Hear the Thunder of Cascading Waterfalls . . . . . . . . . . . . . . . . . 64

**51.** Score a Home Run of Fun at a Syracuse Mets Game . . . . . . . . . . 66

**52.** Step Outside Your Comfort Zone at Canyon Climb Adventure . . . 67

**53.** Learn Why Conservation Matters at the Rosamond Gifford Zoo . . 68

**54.** Seek Serenity in Upper Onondaga Park . . . . . . . . . . . . . . . . . . . . 70

**55.** Rev Up Your Engine at the Syracuse Nationals . . . . . . . . . . . . . . . 71

**56.** Bliss Out at Baltimore Woods and Sycamore Hill Gardens . . . . . . 72

**57.** Break the Ice with Fans at a Syracuse Crunch Game . . . . . . . . . . 73

**58.** Rock Around the Lake at Clark Reservation . . . . . . . . . . . . . . . . . 74

**59.** Putter an Afternoon Away at Fairmount Glen Miniature Golf . . . . 75

**60.** Try Something New at Onondaga County Parks . . . . . . . . . . . . . . 76

## Culture and History

**61.** Become a Syracuse Wise Guy at the OHA . . . . . . . . . . . . . . . . . . 80

**62.** See Green at the Upside-Down Traffic Light . . . . . . . . . . . . . . . . 81

**63.** Admire American Art at the Everson Museum . . . . . . . . . . . . . . . 82

• • • • • • • • • • • • • • • • • • • • • • • • • • • • • •

**64.** Travel Back in Time with the Downtown Historic Walking Tour ... 83

**65.** Practice Gratitude at Skä•noñh, the Great Law of Peace Center.... 84

**66.** Revisit America's Historic Waterway at the Erie Canal Museum ... 85

**67.** Play Out Your Period Drama at Lorenzo State Historic Site...... 86

**68.** Ask Where They "Get Their Ideas" at the Gifford Author Series ... 87

**69.** Feed Your Brain at the MOST............................ 88

**70.** Wax Eloquent on Quarter-Sawn Oak and All Things Stickley .... 89

**71.** Make the City Your Oyster atop the Hotel Syracuse............ 90

**72.** Change Your Mind at Art Galleries Amplifying Diverse Voices ... 91

**73.** Trace the Underground Railroad through Syracuse's
Freedom Trail......................................... 92

**74.** Climb University Hill for Music, Art, and Roses .............. 94

**75.** Wander the Gallery-without-Walls that is Stone Quarry
Hill Art Park.......................................... 95

**76.** Book a Tour or Ghost Walk at Oakwood Cemetery ............ 96

**77.** Count Down Summer at Cultural Festivals at Area Churches..... 98

**78.** Meet the Mother-in-Law of Oz at the
Matilda Joslyn Gage House ............................ 100

**79.** Go with the Flow along Creekwalk....................... 102

**80.** Find Your Muse at the YMCA's Downtown Writers Center..... 103

**81.** Put Yourself in the Picture with Syracuse Street Art.......... 104

**Shopping and Fashion**

**82.** Buy Local, Gift Thoughtful at Salt City Artisans ............. 108

**83.** Join the Cult-like Fans of Wegmans Grocery Store ........... 109

**84.** Rally 'Round Women-Owned Retail in Marcellus ............ 110

**85.** Take the Stairs at the Syracuse Antique Exchange . . . . . . . . . . . . 112

**86.** Become a Locavore at the CNY Regional Market. . . . . . . . . . . . 113

**87.** Brave No-Frills Buda's for Rock-Bottom Prices . . . . . . . . . . . . . . 114

**88.** Support the ARTpreneurs of Wildflowers Armory . . . . . . . . . . . . 115

**89.** Go Underground for the Eclectic Shops of McCarthy Mercantile. . 116

**90.** Remark on the Rose-y Similarities of H. Grey Supply Co. . . . . . . 117

**91.** Glow Up at Syracuse Fashion Week . . . . . . . . . . . . . . . . . . . . . . . 118

**92.** Ooh and Aah at the Syracuse Arts and Crafts Festival . . . . . . . . . 119

**93.** Drive Out for the Farm-Fresh Charm of 20 East. . . . . . . . . . . . . . 120

**94.** Meet the Makers at Shop Small Sunday . . . . . . . . . . . . . . . . . . . . 121

**95.** Bring Home the Luck of the Irish from Cashel House . . . . . . . . . 122

**96.** Browse the Charming Boutiques of Historic Cazenovia . . . . . . . . 123

**97.** Shop A to Z inside Mega-Mall Destiny USA . . . . . . . . . . . . . . . . 124

**98.** Unearth a Treasure at Amanda Bury Antiques . . . . . . . . . . . . . . . 125

**99.** Wheel and Deal at the Sunday Flea Market. . . . . . . . . . . . . . . . . . 126

**100.** Get into the Holiday Spirit at These Seasonal Markets . . . . . . . . 128

**Suggested Itineraries** . . . . . . . . . . . . . . . . . . . . . . . . . . . . . . . . . . . . 130

**Activities by Season** . . . . . . . . . . . . . . . . . . . . . . . . . . . . . . . . . . . . . 137

**Index** . . . . . . . . . . . . . . . . . . . . . . . . . . . . . . . . . . . . . . . . . . . . . . . . . 141

# ACKNOWLEDGMENTS

A city without people is a theater stage without players: no life, no action, no story—just setting. This book lives and breathes because of the following exceptional people.

Phil Memmer for the chance. Debbie Horan for trust. Michelle Kivisto for belief, Sora Iriye for love. Mr. and Mrs. Deep Throat Syracuse—Barbara and Bob Bachmann—for the inside scoop. Michael John Heagerty for assistance, vision, and enthusiasm. Photographer Sandy Roe for her extraordinary eye and generosity. Dongmin Shin for "seeing" Syracuse. Kelley Romano for eagles, baseball, and peerless editing. Judy Carr for Tip Hill and sunsets. Carole Horan for that dinner suggestion. Beta readers Aaron Perrine, Nathan McCarty, and especially Cynthia Kieber-King. Angela Kaufman for insight. Alexis Pierce for purpose, Santosh David for peace. Jane Purden for that Piseco summer pause.

Also Dianne Apter, Leslie Archer, Sharon Akkoul, Stephanie Bartling, Emily Bragdon, Charlene Brusso, Danielle Benjamin, Rita Craner, Steve Carlic, Maureen Curtin, Leila Dean, Evelyn Fiorenza, Jessica Flood, Blair Frodelius, Susan Hynds, Phyllis Ilnitzki, Tim Kivisto, Kathy Miller, Charlie Miller, Lois Needham, Nora O'Dea, Georgia Popoff, and Kristina Starowitz for thoughts that shaped this book. For the hiatus, AWC Pod People not mentioned above—Alice Barden,

* * * * * * * * * * * * * * * * * * * * * * * * * *

Amanda Blue, Andra Brill, Lacey Roy, Lynne Kemen, Dyann Nashton, Julene Waffle, Vicki Whicker, Laurey Williams—I did it, you can too. And Larry West for that first chance. (Apologies to anyone I overlooked.)

Most of all to Jim, Jo, and Mia for letting me disappear into this book: 11 weeks of madness and mayhem, no cooking, cleaning, housekeeping—but many meals out, many places visited. You three are the head, heart, and soul of everything I write. Finally, Reedy Press for backing this production: Metro Syracuse's very own travel guidebook, at last! Raise the curtain on CNY. Let's show the world what we've got.

# PREFACE

You know the saying, "A stranger is a friend you haven't met"? Cities are like that: just a dot on the map until you arrive. Welcome to Syracuse: large enough to be interesting, small enough that there hasn't been a tourist / travel guidebook specific to our city until now. Let's get you acquainted.

We're known as Central New York because Syracuse is the bullseye of the Empire State. At the crossroads of two major travel routes (the NYS Thruway and Interstate 81), we're convenient to the Adirondack and Catskill Mountains (each only two hours away), the Great Lakes, and the Finger Lakes. And with New York City four hours in one direction and Niagara Falls three hours in the other, we're the perfect midway point for the estimated 8 million tourists who travel between those top two attractions each year.

We're the Salt City because back in the 19th century, Onondaga Lake's briny springs were boiled down to produce salt. Today we're known for basketball and snow, the former thanks to Syracuse University's winningest coach, Jim Boeheim, the latter because we're #1 nationally for the most snowfall in a metropolitan area per year. We routinely win New York State's annual Golden Snowball Award—we average 10 feet a year and once topped out at 16 feet. So, we love our coffee to stay

• • • • • • • • • • • • • • • • • • • • • • • • • •

warm, our beer to stay cool, and our festivals to keep the heart of downtown lively in all kinds of weather.

And every year at the end of August, at the western edge of the city, we host the Great New York State Fair, the East Coast's biggest end-of-summer blast: 13 days of midway rides, music, and magic enjoyed by 1.3 million attendees. That number—twice our metro area population of 660,000—makes us swell with pride because the Fair is uniquely Syracuse.

And that's what's in these pages: not the "best of" but the places, faces, and spaces that can only be found in or near Syracuse. If you want rankings and competition, you've got Tripadvisor and Yelp. If you want a friend to show you around, here I am.

• • • • • • • • • • • • • • • • • • • • • • • • • • •

# FOOD AND DRINK

# ANTICIPATE WHILE YOU WAIT
## AT DINOSAUR BAR-B-QUE

Wear white at your peril. This restaurant, blues venue, and biker bar—named America's best barbecue by *Good Morning America*—doesn't serve knife-and-fork food, so don't be dainty: keep napkins nearby. The St. Louis ribs are dry-rubbed and slow-smoked. The brisket—Certified Angus Beef Prime—is aged for 30 days and hand-sliced. The pulled pork is fork tender, the chicken apple-brined and pit-smoked; both are moist, their deep flavors complemented by the Dino's original sauce. Order a Combo Plate and choose between the aforementioned four-plus spicy shrimp boil or jalapeño cheddar hot sausage. Pick your sides—cornbread is included. You'll wait for a table, but the food arrives lickety-split. Now a six-restaurant empire, Syracuse was the first and it's still the best.

246 W. Willow St., 315-476-4937
dinosaurbarbque.com/syracuse

# SAVOR GLOBAL GOODIES
## AT SALT CITY MARKET

Travel around the world in eighty bites at this 24,000-square-foot public market. Food stalls offer menus developed from original recipes and heritage dishes based on cultural traditions. Find Middle Eastern, Jamaican, Caribbean, Burmese, Thai, Vietnamese, Southern (US), and soul food cuisine here, run by women and entrepreneurs of color. There are also sweet and savory pies, cakes and cupcakes, juices and fresh flowers. Syracuse Cooperative Market has a well-stocked grocery store with whole, local, and organic foods, and Salt City Bar—a café with a twist—serves innovative cocktails, beer, wine, and creative coffee. Folks are taking notice of Salt City Market, not just locally but nationally. In 2021, Fodor's Travel named it one of the ten best new food halls across the US.

484 S. Salina St., 315-401-4111
saltcitymarket.com

Syracuse Cooperative Market
315-552-0029, syracuse.coop

Salt City Bar
315-888-918, saltcitybar.co

---

### TIP

Can't decide what to eat? Baghdad Restaurant's Shawarma Salad is a heaping plateful of crisp greens, vegetables, and protein. Choose either beef or chicken for a tasty meal at just $7.99—a satisfying bang for your buck.

---

# FALL FOR HOT TOM
## AT PASTABILITIES

How do you get Guy Fieri—Food Network's culinary rock star—to shut up? Put Pastabilities Spicy Hot Tomato Oil and Stretch Bread in front of him. "That's crazy!" he told owner Karyn Korteling between mouthfuls on *Diners, Drive-Ins, and Dives*, Season 16, Episode 2. "You need a special license to serve that!" No, you don't. Just order a meal and they'll bring it to you instead of bread and butter. Their Wicked Chicken Riggies are so good the recipe's online at FoodNetwork.com. For a milder version, Turn Down Riggies cuts the heat with added alfredo sauce. If you're in a rush, Pasta's Daily Bread across the street sells Stretch Bread and Spicy Hot Tomato Oil. And when you run out back home, order online at HotTom.com.

311 S. Franklin St., 315-474-1153
pastabilities.com

Pasta's Daily Bread
308 S. Franklin St., 315-701-0224
pastabilities.com/bread

## TIP
For parties of 8-12, call in advance and reserve the Mural Room, an intimate tiny dining space strung with colored lights. Just big enough for a long table and chairs, it features festive revelers hand-painted on the walls.

# CROWN THE CHAMP
## OF CHICKEN RIGGIES

Ready for a culinary rumble? Syracuse and nearby Utica fight about who can rightfully call this signature dish their own. It's a simple recipe: peppers and chicken star in a spicy cream sauce with a touch of tomato served over rigatoni. Native to Central New York, this is the entree every Italian restaurant puts its own spin on. While you could spend weeks sampling dozens of entrees, these three are worth seeking out. Francesca's riggies are buttery with bell peppers, and they offer a seafood version. Attilio's uses chopped cherry peppers, homemade marinara sauce, and scallions. At Nestico's, a red sauce mixed with cream includes hot and sweet peppers, and if you want your riggies gluten free, just ask.

Francesca's Cucina
545 N. Salina St., 315-425-1556
francescas-cucina.com

Attilio's
770 James St., 315-218-5085
attiliosonjames.com

Nestico's
412 N. Main St., North Syracuse
315-458-5188
nesticosrestaurant.com

---

### TIP
The best chicken riggies? Serious foodies claim the Cinderella story coming out of nowhere is Green Lakes Lanes—yes, a bowling alley! Unusual ingredients like sherry-marinated chicken, cream cheese, and tomato soup will topple your expectations.

# CUISINE-HOP
## IN ARMORY SQUARE

A once seedy section of town now transformed into a National Historic District, this urban neighborhood is as attractive as it is trendy. With more bars and restaurants than any other part of town—many in architecturally significant buildings—Armory Square is Syracuse's premier date-night destination. When planning your visit, it's helpful to know that Walton Street—one of two main thoroughfares—is closed to vehicular traffic on Fridays and Saturdays. Within a two-block radius are dozens of places to eat and drink. Try Kasai Ramen for Japanese noodle bowls. One block north, Kitty Hoynes is a traditional Irish pub serving traditional Irish grub; lunches are leisurely, evenings are packed. At white-tablecloth Lemon Grass, Pacific Rim Thai goes upscale. Bright, mid-century-themed Modern Malt elevates diner comfort food and serves artisanal cocktails.

Kasai Ramen
218 Walton St., 315-310-8500
kasairamen.com

Lemon Grass
113 Walton St., 315-475-1111
lemongrasscny.com

Kitty Hoynes Irish Pub
301 W. Fayette St., 315-424-1974
kittyhoynes.com

Modern Malt
323 S. Clinton St., 315-471-6258
eatdrinkmalt.com

## TIP

Isn't it romantic? For over 30 years, Armory Square has hosted the Candlelight Series: free outdoor concerts held in July and August. On those nights, streets in the Square are closed to vehicular traffic at 4 p.m., giving restaurants time to offer patrons fine outdoor candlelight dining before the concert begins.

Corner of W. Jefferson and Franklin Sts.

armorysq.org

# TOAST THE KNIGHTS OF NI
## AT MIDDLE AGES BREWING

If Monty Python had an official beverage, this granddaddy of New York State microbreweries would produce it. Marc and Mary Rubenstein founded the brewery in 1995, and initially Britannia ruled the waves of beer they produced, primarily English-style ales. As fans of Monty Python's *Holy Grail* movie, they named their brews accordingly: two longtime favorites are ImPaled Ale—one of their first IPAs—and The Duke of Winship, a well-loved porter. Middle Ages uses malted barley imported from England and a house yeast that originated there. Sour ales, milkshake IPAs, coffee stouts, and New England (hazy) IPAs are more recent additions. The beer hall/tasting room features over two dozen beers on tap. Enter through the medieval front door—safe passage is guaranteed, even if you forget to bring a nice, not-too-expensive shrubbery.

20 Wilkinson St., 315-476-4250
middleagesbrewing.com

---

### TIP
Mark your calendar for Middle Ages' big annual outdoor party—its Anniversary Celebration—on the first Sunday of August at Leavenworth Park across from the brewery. Live music all day, with food and drink for purchase.

---

# BREAKFAST 'TIL YOU BURST
## AT MOTHER'S CUPBOARD

Pancakes bigger than your head. Frittatas to feed you for days. The mother of all hole-in-the-wall diners was a well-kept secret until 2010. That's when the Travel Channel taped an episode of *Man v Food*. Host Adam Richman downed the diner's signature frittata, a six-pound scramble of eggs, sausage, pepperoni, peppers, and potatoes, putting Mother's on the foodie map. Though its reputation has grown, it hasn't put on airs. The redwood-sided shack still sits at the edge of a dirt parking lot surrounded by towering trees. It's still tiny at just 30 seats. If you have to wait, it won't be long because the friendly, energetic staff really hustles to get the orders out. Your plate—then you—will groan with food. Get a take-home container—there will be leftovers.

3709 E. James St., 315-432-0942

facebook.com/motherscupboardsyr

---

### TIP
Finish the full-size fritatta and you'll get your photo on the wall in the Mother's Cupboard Hall of Fame. Thousands have tried; most have failed.

---

# TRADE BLARNEY
## AT COLEMAN'S AUTHENTIC IRISH PUB

On the west side of Syracuse, midway up Tipperary Hill ("Tipp Hill" to locals), is a stately green clapboard building. Coleman's, the heart of this close-knit neighborhood, was established in 1933 by Peter A. Coleman as a workingman's pub. When he became ill, his 18-year-old son stepped in and the business took off. Young Peter not only expanded the pub but became the community's biggest booster, establishing Green Beer Sunday and raising funds for Stone Thrower's Park, a monument to Irish immigrants. Coleman's is venerable with polished woodwork and stained glass windows, but also playful—look for a window depicting the neighborhood's famous upside-down stoplight. Outside, there's another bit of fun: two doors, one for humans and one for leprechauns—a wee one at 15 inches tall.

100 S. Lowell Ave., 315-476-1933
colemansirishpub.com

---

### TIP
Of course, you'll order the Irish specialties: Beef O'Flaherty (roast beef with homemade bleu cheese dressing), bangers and mash, fish and chips, corned beef and cabbage, shepherd's pie, and Guinness Beef Stew.

---

# STUFF YOURSELF SILLY
## AT THE NEW YORK STATE FAIR

Eat like a local with these Fair favorites. Start with the sausage sandwich loaded with peppers and onions (preferably with Gianelli sausage). In 2000 a Senate candidate refused one and later lost the election. Coincidence? We think not! Then stand in line for the Fair's two best deals: the baked potato (regular or sweet) for one dollar, and a cup of NYS milk (white or chocolate) for 25 cents. If you're of legal drinking age, get a wine slushie. Visit the triangle-fronted Villa Pizze Fritte for a two-foot-long stretch of fried pizza dough rolled in sugar. If you are still hungry, search the Midway for the year's latest deep-fried craze (tamer choices have included pickles, Snickers, Twinkies, and a Reese's Cup stuffed between two Double-Stuf Oreos). Extra points if you walk while you eat.

581 State Fair Blvd., 315-487-7711
nysfair.ny.gov

# CAFFEINATE AND COWORK
## AT CAFÉ KUBAL

Java up and hunker down with free Wi-Fi, then settle in at this favorite meeting spot. Local coffee culture is rich across Kubal's seven cafés—all distinctly different—each reflecting the neighborhood vibe. Downtown at the Salina Café, chill under high tin ceilings and chandeliers, while at Creekwalk Commons, gawk at the Art Deco details of the Niagara Mohawk building across the street. There are the usual green, black, white, and herbal teas, plus a silky coconut oolong. Breakfast bagels and burritos, lunchtime sandwiches and wraps—along with scones, cookies, and sweets—round out the menu. If you need a quiet space for zoom or webinar meetings, upstairs at Hawley Green is Kubal Coworks, where a day pass includes office/desk space, a green screen, and other telecommuting amenities. Work it, baby!

**Hawley Green Café**
208 N. Townsend St., 315-422-2936

**Salina Café**
401 S. Salina St., 315-440-6441

**Eastwood Café**
3501 James St., 315-278-2812

**Upstate Golisano Children's Hospital Café**
1 Children's Circle, 315-876-1259

**Creekwalk Commons Café**
324 W. Water St.

**Sweetheart Corners Café + Drive-thru**
3911 Brewerton Rd., North Syracuse

**Manlius Café**
343 Fayette St., Manlius, 315-692-2010

shop.cafekubal.com

# CIRCLE HANOVER SQUARE
## FOR BREAKFAST, LUNCH, AND DINNER

Just below the State Tower Building—Syracuse's tallest—you'll find Hanover Square. The neighborhood is home to some of the city's toniest apartments and restaurants. The Sweet Praxis has breakfast sandwiches, baked goods, hand pies, and Frenchest toast (orange zest syrup, apricot preserves, and almond frangipane), plus vegan donuts named among the nation's best by PETA. Praxis's large glass windows front an entire city block, making it perfect for people watching. The Fish Friar next to City Hall—open for lunch and dinner—specializes in fresh wild-caught seafood from coastal Maine. Nearby, atmospheric Otro Cinco focuses on Spanish tapas for dinner. At intimate Eden, locally sourced ingredients means the wood-fired entrees change with the seasons; from presentation to service, they offer the culinary equivalent of fine art.

The Sweet Praxis
203 E. Water St., 315-216-7797
thesweetpraxis.com

Otro Cinco
206 S. Warren St., 315-422-6876
otro5cinco.com

The Fish Friar
110 Montgomery St., 315-468-FISH
thefishfriar.com

Eden
118 E. Genesee St., 315-991-8408
edencny.com

# PICK APPLES AND MORE
## AT BEAK & SKIFF AND 1911 ESTABLISHED

*USA Today* proclaims it the nation's best apple orchard. Once a rustic hilltop farm, the Beak & Skiff/1911 Established Apple Campus is now an agri-tourism destination. Just like college, the Campus buildings open in September. The Café sells burgers, wraps, and salads, and the Bakery is everything apple: pies, crisps, dumplings, donuts, candy, and caramel apples. The Fritter Shack focuses on apple fritters, hot and fresh. The General Store has cider and homemade fudge along with gorgeous gift items. The Tavern and Tasting Room offers 1911 Established premium small batch spirits: bourbon, vodka, brandy, whisky, gin—think Honeycrisp Vodka and Cider Donut Bourbon. Visit the Apple Barn to take home a bag or bushel, but for the real experience, stroll the picturesque orchard and pick your own.

Beak & Skiff
2708 Lord's Hill Rd. (Rte. 80), Lafayette
beakandskiff.com

1911 Established Distillery
4473 Cherry Valley Tpke. (US Rte. 20), Lafayette
1911established.com

# DECIDE THE DINER THROW-DOWN
## OVER THE FRETTA

You say tomato, I say frittata . . . or frettata . . . or fretta. Among three popular diners, each has its own name for what non-Syracusans call an Italian omelet. It's a combination of eggs, home fries, sausage, pepperoni, onions, peppers, mushrooms, and broccoli, but instead of letting the eggs set during cooking, they're scrambled. At Stella's it's called a *fretta*, and they add ham to the mix. At the Gem Diner, a Syracuse institution for over 70 years, it's a *fretatta*, but they leave out the mushrooms. The Market Diner calls it a *frittata*, and they're all about transparency: they use local Gianelli sausage, caramelized onions, both red and green peppers, three eggs for a half order, five for a huge order. At all three, add cheese for an extra buck.

Stella's Diner North
110 Wolf St., 315-425-0353
stellasdinersyracuse.com

The Gem Diner
832 Spencer St., 315-314-7380
thegemdiner.com

The Market Diner
2100 Park St., 315-474-5247
themarketdiner.com

# SURRENDER TO FLAVOR
## AT THE CIDER MILL

This apple-red building—tucked into the hillside of a residential neighborhood—looks unprepossessing. The interior is equally modest. Don't, however, judge a dining room by its decor: these folks catered Food Network chef Anne Burrell's October 2021 wedding. When the food comes, the first bite demands attention. The Truffle Parmesan Chicken Wing starter is crispy, garlicky, bone-gnawingly good; the Miso Glazed Salmon—delicate and delicious. The chicken chunks in the Chicken Riggies are marvelously tender. Even the vegetable sides have snap and savor. Evidence of the building's former life as Morey's Mill graces the dining room (an old menu is painted on the previous owner's headboard). Moderate prices and nothing fancy-schmancy: don't come here to see or be seen. It's the food—precise preparation, nuanced flavor—simply delightful.

4221 Fay Rd., 315-487-0647
thecidermill.us

# HOLLER AT WHAT A DOLLAR GETS YOU
## AT TASTE OF SYRACUSE

This annual two-day festival is the city's unofficial kickoff to summer, typically held the first Friday and Saturday in June. It's a big deal for three reasons: One: it packs Clinton Square with over 200,000 foodies. Two: it's cheap because of the festival's unique premise—every vendor has to offer a "taste" for just a buck. That means you can sample bang bang shrimp, bacon-wrapped meatballs, jerk chicken kabobs, gourmet egg rolls, fried calamari, haddock bites, mac 'n cheese baked potatoes, double chocolate brownies, or waffles on a stick for just one dollar. Three: each year it brings a national headliner to perform—think Cheap Trick, Marshall Tucker Band, or Brett Michaels. Plus, you can also get beer and wine slushies—but of course those cost a bit more.

Clinton Square
315-471-9597
tasteofsyracuse.com

## TIP

The ultimate must-eat food is
the Salt Potato, a Salty City spin on potatoes
boiled in salted water. According to urban
legend surrounding this local specialty, in the
1800s Irish salt workers would bring small
potatoes from home, boil them in the area's
naturally occurring brine, and eat 'em for
lunch. The heavy concentration of salt forms
a crusty surface. An acquired taste,
they're puckery good.

# *MANGIA* OLD WORLD SPECIALTIES
## IN LITTLE ITALY

Tradition endures on the Northside, reflecting the neighborhood's immigrant heritage. Here, foods you won't find elsewhere are a part of daily life. Biscotti's tiered cases display cakes, cookies, cannolis, and pastries in ruffled baking cups, flaky layers enfolding sweet cream. Try the lobster claw filled with mascarpone; take home some icy cold gelato. At Columbus, they only sell Italian bread, the best in the city. Point, flat, and sandwich loaves are baked in tiled ovens dating back to 1897; ask for one right out of the oven. Avoiding carbs? Liehs & Steigerwald is a classic butcher shop selling hand-cut steaks, chops, roasts, sausages, beef tongue, and even goose and rabbit, wrapped in white paper. Lombardi's has Italian and European foods, delicacies, housewares, and an extensive selection of stovetop espresso pots. Buon appetito!

Biscotti Café and Gelateria
741 N. Salina St., 315-478-9583
biscotticafe.com

Columbus Baking Co.
502 Pearl St., 315-422-2913
facebook.com/Columbus-Baking-
CompanyColumbus-Meats-and-
Cheeses-117096361651397

Liehs and Steigerwald
1857 Grant Blvd., 315-474-2171
liehsandsteigerwald.com

Lombardi's Imports
534 Butternut St., 315-472-5900
facebook.com/LombardisImports

## TIP

The hottest spot in Little Italy is Habiba's
Ethiopian Kitchen. As a child, Habiba learned
to cook in a refugee camp in Kenya. She came
to Syracuse at age 14 and opened her restaurant
at 32, fulfilling a lifelong dream.

656 N. Salina St., 315-299-4099
habibaskitchen.com

# RISK BRAIN FREEZE
## AT GANNON'S ICE CREAM

With roughly three dozen flavors to choose from, don't even think about approaching the window before you decide—you don't want to hold up the line. That's not even counting soft serve, yogurt, Dole Whip, custard, sherbet, or sorbet. Gannon's small-batch ice cream is homemade, so new combinations routinely debut. View their rotating list of 200 flavors online, all coded by availability: Always, Frequently, Occasionally, Rarely, Seasonally, Retired. Seasonal favorites include Apple Crisp, apple ice cream with brown sugar crisps; and Peach Cobbler, peach ice cream with pie crust pieces. Always available: Chocolate Raspberry Truffle—chocolate ice cream, raspberry swirl, and chocolate cookie crumbles. Eat inside for the added treat of hippy drippy murals, furnishings, and wall art painted by cartoonist J.P. Crangle.

1525 Valley Dr., 315-469-8647
gannonsicecream.com

# DINE INN STYLE
## AT A CAZENOVIA LANDMARK

If these walls could talk. Eat, drink, and soak in the atmosphere of three 19th-century estates in this quaint lakeside village. Their combined history totals over 500 years of elegance. The Linklaen House, "The Oldest Grand Hotel in Central New York," first opened in 1836. Built by village founder John Linklaen, it has hosted former presidents and oil barons. The main dining room is posh, but if you are looking for something more casual, head down to the cozy Seven Stone Steps Tap Room for their legendary popovers. Three blocks away, an 1805 mansion has been home to the Scottish-themed Brae Loch Inn since 1950. Of course, they serve Guinness steak pie and haggis. The opulent Brewster Inn, a Gilded-Age mansion on Cazenovia Lake, is an award-winning special-occasion restaurant. All three offer lodging as well.

Linklaen House
79 Albany St., Cazenovia
315-655-3461, linklaenhouse.com

The Brae Loch Inn
5 Cazenovia St., Cazenovia
315-655-3431, braelochinn.com

The Brewster Inn
6 Ledyard Ave., Cazenovia, 315-655-9232
thebrewsterinn.com

# POLISH OFF
# A POLISH FEAST
## AT EVA'S

Even if DNA testing says otherwise, you've got a Polish ciotka (aunt) eager to serve you authentic food in her homey restaurant. Eva Zaczynski's menu features Polskie Specjaly (Polish Specialties): eight kinds of Pierogi (filled dumplings) including potato, sauerkraut and bacon, meat, sweet cheese, and blueberry; Golabki (cabbage rolls stuffed with ground beef); Kielbasa (sausage); Placki (potato pancakes); Kopytka (potato dumplings); Bigos (Hunter's Stew); and Gulasz (goulash). They also offer Salatki (salads) like leek and red cabbage, and Polish, Ukrainian, Russian, and German beer. Three dining areas are chock-full of hand-painted folk art like matryoshka dolls. In warm weather, colorful murals carry the theme to the outdoor dining area. Of course, you'll want to order one of Eva's homemade desserts—the Orange Chocolate Ganache is fantastyczny (fantastic). Na zdrowie (cheers)!

1305 Milton Ave., 315-487-2722
evaspolish.com

---

### TIP
If you're asked, "Do you want the homemade mustard?" say yes! Eva makes a cream-colored condiment with robust heat that'll wake up your kielbasa; it's a whole new level of deliciousness.

---

# WOLF A DOG OR CONEY
## AT HEID'S

This Art Deco mecca for fast food is an architectural landmark—or folly—with "Food You'll Like" in large blue letters, porthole windows, and chrome trim. Little has changed over the decades, yet lines still form for those made-in-Syracuse dogs. Not just a hot dog, but a Hofmann Frank (containing beef, pork, and veal) or a Snappy (a Coney with pork and veal, startlingly white because it contains no artificial colors). Choose from a dozen toppings including onions, gravy, relish, mushrooms, and of course, sauerkraut. It's narrow and cramped inside Heid's—that's part of the charm. Order at one end of the steel counter, shuffle down to pick up your food, then follow the L-turn to the condiments table. Don't splash mustard, though everyone does.

305 Oswego St., Liverpool, 315-451-0786
heidsofliverpool.com

---

## TIP

After you load up on condiments, exit the building and go around to re-enter the dining room at the other end, or eat outside at picnic tables under the red-and-white awning in spring through fall. Whatever you do, don't ignore the one-way floor signs and push past the queue—that exposes you as a rude first-timer.

# RAISE A GLASS TO FREEDOM
## AT LUNA LOCA

It's a church . . . a restaurant . . . a way station on the Underground Railroad. Today, this Tex-Mex cantina-style bar and eatery enchants on looks alone: stained glass windows, overhead string lanterns, a seductive man-in-the-moon mural. But below its California-cool surface lies an unsolved mystery. Deep in a subterranean passage tunneled from rock, this former Wesleyan Methodist Church sheltered enslaved people escaping to freedom. Faces found sculpted into the walls may have been their work. While those artifacts have been removed and are now on display at the Onondaga Historical Association, you can still toast their spirit with a Luna Blanca sangria or a blood orange jalapeño margarita, one of six different flavors. A ramp at the back door makes the restaurant fully accessible. Let freedom ring!

304-310 E. Onondaga St., 315-475-0913
lunalocasyr.com

# HEAD TO THE HILLS
## FOR MICROBREWS AND VIEWS

Unwind with a cold one out on the farm. A short drive away, three rural microbreweries are open year-round with food and live music. Local 315's compact barn has a cozy tap room and outdoor picnic tables. They grow their own hops, make friendly farm animals available to the kids, and bring in food trucks on weekends. From high atop breezy Heritage Hill, the view of downtown Syracuse and Onondaga Lake is jaw-dropping. With a playground, hammock swings, huge barn/deck, and sunset happy hour, it's wildly popular. Meier's Creek is the most sophisticated of the three, its interior a blend of industrial-chic and ski-lodge styles. Outside, awning-covered seating and Adirondack chairs overlook a plush lawn and wooded hillside. Play disc golf while you charge your hybrid vehicle for free.

| Local 315 Brewing | Heritage Hill Brewhouse | Meier's Creek Brewing |
|---|---|---|
| 3160 Warners Rd. | 3149 Sweet Rd., | 33 Rippleton Rd. |
| Warners, 315-468-2337 | Pompey, 315-468-2337 | Cazenovia, 315-815-4022 |
| local315brewing.com | heritagehillbrewery.com | meierscreekbrewing.com |

---

### TIP

Heritage Hill is home of the new Brewseum, a beer museum curated in collaboration with the Onondaga Historical Association. It's like a school field trip for adults 21 and over, but instead of a chaperone, bring along a designated driver.

cnyhistory.org/explore/the-brewseum-at-heritage-hill

---

# MUSIC
# AND ENTERTAINMENT

# BE ONE IN A MILLION
## AT THE GREAT NEW YORK STATE FAIR

The New York State Fair is held the last 13 days of summer through Labor Day. See free concerts at two great venues—big-name entertainers at the 15-acre Chevy Park, and country, nostalgia, and pop/rock musicians at the 3-acre Chevy Court. Grab a bag at Guest Relations and collect freebies. Marvel at the Fair's two iconic sculptures, one from butter, one from sand. Enjoy kiddie rides at the Family Fun Zone or sit for your caricature. Coo over silkie chickens in the Poultry Barn or photobomb TV news anchors broadcasting live. Feed a monarch inside the butterfly garden or witness new life at the Dairy Cow Birthing Center. You can also follow product demonstrations at the Center of Progress Building. With an Unlimited Ride armband, scream aboard 50+ midway rides—but don't eat beforehand. And when your legs give out, catch the free tram.

581 State Fair Blvd., 315-487-7711
nysfair.ny.gov

# REVEL IN THE DAZZLE
## OF THE LANDMARK THEATRE

This theatrical palace—with walls of gilt and other ornamentation, glittering chandeliers, filigreed balconies, and plush red seating (new in 2021)—is opulent, exotic, and otherworldly. First opened in 1928, it was designed by noted architect Thomas Lamb, named a "king of theaters" by the *New York Times*. It was saved from the wrecking ball in 1977 by concerned citizens under the acronym SALT: Syracuse Area Landmark Theatre. Today, Broadway touring productions, concerts, comedy, family shows, and even private events fill the lobby and theater. The Landmark's ongoing restoration will be complete by its centennial celebration in 2028, and in the meantime, annual events like the holiday showing of *It's a Wonderful Life* and the Landmark fundraising gala—which involves miniature golf played throughout the theater—provide financial support for this Syracuse showpiece.

362 S. Salina St., 315-475-7979
landmarktheatre.org

---

## TIP

Broadway in Syracuse/Famous Artists brings national touring companies to the Landmark for multi-day runs. *Hamilton*, *Wicked*, and Disney's *The Lion King* have all played sold-out shows here.

374 S. Salina St., 315-424-8210, broadwayinsyracuse.com

---

# KEEP THE DOCTOR AWAY
## AT THE LAFAYETTE APPLE FESTIVAL

We know what a daily apple is good for; so, what is the benefit of attending a two-day apple extravaganza in early October? Maybe it's the enjoyment of the live music, hot apple fritters, amusement rides, scarecrow competition, or simply the celebration of small-town life in this rural community just south of Syracuse. Every Columbus Day weekend, 30,000 attendees take Route 20 down to Apple Valley for the festival. The event is a successful fundraiser for local civic organizations who prepare food for the hungry hordes. Favorites include stuffed baked potatoes, chicken spiedies, hot sausage sandwiches, and apple treats from caramel apples to apple popcorn. At two local churches, volunteers lovingly bake—and sell—thousands of apple pies. Plus, with over 400 vendors, it's an arts-and-crafts lover's dream.

5330 Rowland Rd., Lafayette, 315-677-3498
lafayetteapplefest.org

# BAUM AROUND
## OZ-STRAVAGANZA AND ALL THINGS OZ

There's no place like the home of L. Frank Baum: Chittenango, where in 1856 the *Wonderful Wizard of Oz* author was born. Just east of Syracuse, the village is a mecca for Baum fans and Oz enthusiasts, both for its All Things Oz Museum and its annual three-day Oz-Stravaganza in June. The longest-running and largest Oz-themed festival in the world, Oz-Stravaganza has hosted several of the MGM movie's original Munchkins as well as Academy and Grammy Award–winning composer Stephen Schwartz, who penned the songs for Broadway's blockbuster musical *Wicked*. The parade and autograph sessions draw big crowds, many in Oz character costumes. Open year-round, the All Things Oz Museum exhibits over a thousand pieces of Oz memorabilia, including original props and costumes.

Oz-Stravaganza
Genesee St., Chittenango
oz-stravaganza.com

All Things Oz Museum
219 Genesee St., Chittenango, 315-687-7772
allthingsoz.org/all-things-oz-museum.html

# IMMERSE YOURSELF
## IN THE OTHERWORLDLY MUSEUM OF INTRIGUE

Imagine during a trip to Orlando, Florida, you press pause on a Disneyworld or Universal Studios theme park ride, jump off, and explore the fantastical surroundings. This interactive theatrical gaming experience—the only one of its kind in the world—feels like that. Investigate a dozen scenarios across 9,000 square feet: shipwreck, art gallery, haunted church, cobblestone village, book-lined library, great hall, train car, shadowy laboratory, jungle rainforest, and more. Pick an adventure story. Solve clues; interact with characters; touch, handle, or manipulate objects: there's no time limit and no playing with strangers. The creative team includes a former Universal Studios set designer, a traveling-stage-magician set builder, game designers, and MFA-graduate writers. Plus, they've partnered with KultureCity to adjust stories to meet sensory needs of guests.

Destiny USA (third floor)
306 Hiawatha Blvd., 855-653-7227
intrigueandco.com/museum-of-intrigue

KultureCity
kulturecity.org

## TIP

The museum's creative team is also behind Frightmare Farms, named among New York's best haunted attractions. The world's first certified Sensory Inclusive Haunted Attraction, Frightmare staff are trained to assist customers with autism, anxiety, PTSD, and seizure disorders, and they have kits on-site to help individuals with sensitivity concerns.

4816 State Rt. 49, Palermo, 844-FRIGHT-1
frightmarefarms.net

# TRIPLE YOUR FUN
## AT THE ONCENTER

Look! Southeast of downtown! It's a convention center! It's an arena! It's a multi-theater complex! Like Clark Kent changing into Superman, the Oncenter is Syracuse's most versatile events hub for everything A to Z. From arts performances by civic groups to the Zamboni machine that resurfaces the ice rink, three facilities right next to each other accommodate local and national events. The Civic Center's three theaters feature performances from classical to R&B, comedian Chelsea Handler to Food Network's Alton Brown, and Syracuse Opera. The War Memorial—a three-tiered 7,000-seat venue—hosts Syracuse Crunch hockey, concerts, and even houses a military museum. The Convention Center transforms itself according to purpose: building a 48-lane bowling alley for the annual US Bowling Congress Open Championships then scaling back for high school graduations. The Oncenter is the Supervenue of Central New York, and it doesn't need a phone booth to make a change.

Nicholas J. Pirro Convention Center
800 S. State St.

Upstate Medical Arena
War Memorial
515 Montgomery St.

John H. Mulroy Civic Center Theaters
421 Montgomery St., 315-435-8000
asmsyracuse.com

Military History Museum
War Memorial, 515 Montgomery St.
cnyhistory.org/programs/
war-memorial

# CHOOSE YOUR MUSICAL GROOVE
## AT A SYMPHORIA CONCERT

The Orchestra of Central New York is no ordinary symphony orchestra: this non-profit musician-led cooperative orchestra is just one of two in the US. Symphoria offers five concert series each season. The popular *Masterworks* and *Pops* series are offered in the Civic Center's Crouse-Hinds Theater, a 2,000-seat symphony hall; the other three take place at more intimate venues. *Casual* concerts, held afternoons at St. Paul's Episcopal Cathedral, feature post-performance musician meet-and-greets. *Kids'* concerts, one-hour performances at Inspiration Hall, are free to those under 18. *Spark* is symphony with attitude: past shows have included a costumed October 31 *Poe Halloween* and a circus-style show featuring aerial acrobatics and stunt performances by CirqOvation. Each year their 50-plus concerts reach over 100,000 in CNY.

Crouse-Hinds Theater
411 Montgomery St., 315-299-5598
experiencesymphoria.org

CirqOvation
cirqovation.com

---

## TIP
Give yourself the gift of music, and someone else will benefit as well. With a Symphoria Unlimited single membership at $20 a month, you'll enjoy one ticket to any regular performance, and an adult in need will also receive a Symphoria Unlimited membership.

# DANCE TO LIVE MUSIC
## IN AN ORCHARD AT BEAK & SKIFF

A national concert venue masquerades as an apple orchard in the hills south of Syracuse. Fans come for the big-name performers; the 180-degree views overlooking Lafayette and Apple Valley are an added bonus. Launched in 2016, the Beak & Skiff summer music series began with the Wood Brothers, and has since booked Ani DiFranco, 10,000 Maniacs, Lake Street Dive, the Decemberists, Bruce Hornsby, and Indigo Girls. The natural outdoor amphitheater location can accommodate up to 1,800; bring your own chairs and blankets. (During COVID-19, they sold tickets in two- and four-person PODS—Personal Outdoor Dance Space.) The Friday Night Porch Party is free and held at the 1911 Tasting Room, and down the road at the 1911 Established Distillery building, Music at the Distillery is also free.

Summer Concert Series
2708 Lords Hill Rd. (Rte. 80), Lafayette

Friday Night Porch Party
1911 Tasting Room, 2708 Lords Hill Rd. (Rte. 80), Lafayette

Music at the Distillery
1911 Established Distillery
4473 Cherry Valley Tpke. (US Rte. 20), Lafayette

beakandskiff.com/events/category/music

# ADD DRAMA TO YOUR LIFE
## AT SYRACUSE STAGE

The area's premier professional theater company, Stage (as locals call it) is an Equity theater casting actors from New York City, Chicago, and across the country. Established in 1974, the theater has worked with familiar names like Jason Alexander (*Seinfeld*), Jean Stapleton (*All in the Family*), and John Slattery (*Mad Men*), and it has presented East Coast, American, and world premieres. Each year, Stage collaborates with Syracuse University's School of Drama to produce a family-friendly holiday show that typically sells out: past shows have included Disney's *Beauty and the Beast*, *Elf*, and *Matilda*. Unique to Stage is the Syracuse Stories series, created to foster individual and community change through topics that directly impact the city. Several of these conversations can be viewed on Zoom and YouTube.

820 E. Genesee St., 315-443-3275
syracusestage.org

Syracuse Stories
syracusestage.org/syracusestories.php

---

### TIP
The hot tickets in town for price and value are the Syracuse University Drama Department productions, held in the same theater complex. A top-tier program, SU Drama students often go on to successful careers. According to Playbill, it's #10 in the Most Represented Colleges on Broadway.

vpa.syr.edu/academics/drama/current-season

---

# STRUT YOUR STUFF
## AT THE NYS BLUES FESTIVAL

As one of the largest free blues festivals in the Northeast, the New York State Blues Fest cooks. It's not uncommon for 10,000 blues lovers to show up in Syracuse for this three-day event traditionally held the last weekend in June. The annual festival showcases regional and national artists from a variety of genres. Past names you might recognize include Bo Diddley, Cyril Neville, Little Feat, Little Steven and The Disciples of Soul, Dan Aykroyd, and The Robert Cray Band. Previous venues have included Clinton Square downtown and Chevy Court at the NYS Fairgrounds; the latter benefits from a springy carpet of grass, perfect for spreading a blanket wide. Whatever the location, head up front if you want to dance—performers on stage love to see that.

nysbluesfest.com

# FLY HIGH
## AT THE JAMESVILLE BALLOONFEST

Buoyant envelopes of colorful nylon bobbing overhead—who doesn't love the sight of a hot air balloon . . . or twenty? Watch them lift off at dawn and dusk at this family-friendly weekend festival in June. In between flights, there's live music—more than a dozen acts typically perform—as well as amusement rides, food, drink, fireworks, and a craft fair. Want to go up, up, and away in a beautiful balloon? Make advance reservations for a regular flight or stand in line for a tether flight—a rope holds the balloon in place. Kids and adults can walk inside a partially inflated balloon. This annual event draws as many as 20,000 to the grassy fields at Jamesville Beach Park. It's free with a nominal parking fee.

Jamesville Beach Park
3992 Apulia Rd., Jamesville, 315-703-9620
syracuseballoonfest.com

# PUMP UP THE VOLUME
## AT ST. JOE'S AMP

A lakeview location and capacity for 17,500: at Syracuse's biggest outdoor music venue, warm weather brings national touring acts to town. High on a bluff overlooking Onondaga Lake, the St. Joseph's Health Amphitheater at Lakeview schedules country, rock, pop, hip hop, even kids' concerts from May to October. Purchase general admission lawn access or ticketed seating inside; the 100 section borders the stage, the 300 section has the best lake view from indoors, while lawn seats soak up the sunset. East and West Plazas house restrooms; East Plaza hosts concessions, and food trucks provide more food/beverage options. If you want to avoid post-concert traffic—and you own a boat and don't mind a walk—cruise into the concert and dock at Lakeview Point Landing with a reservation.

490 Restoration Way, 315-435-5100
asmsyracuse.com/p/amphitheater

Lakeview Point Landing, 315-435-8000
dockwa.com/explore/destination/lwce2yj-lakeview-point-landing

---

## TIP
Want to test-drive ticketed seating? When there are no scheduled concerts, the West Shore Trail leads right through St. Joe's Amp, giving you a chance to make like Goldilocks and sample every seat section in the house to find the one that's just right. Park in the Orange Lot and walk the trail to the Amp.

---

# EAT, DRINK, AND CHILL
## AT WINTERFEST

When snow is what you're known for, you make Winterfest out of winter. For 11 days in mid-February, Winterfest celebrates food, fun, and seasonal fortitude. Things always get heated in the annual Chili and Chowder Cook-offs among local restaurants. On the Sandwich Stroll and the Wing Walk, tour eateries, sample items, and vote for your favorite. The Culinary Cruise includes three categories (appetizers, entrees, desserts) in the judging. Then there are cocktail, margarita, and sangria mix-offs and beer judging. The Human Dog Sled Race raises money for local nonprofit Helping Hounds. And for readers of Syracuse's *Post-Standard* newspaper, daily clues in the Winterfest Treasure Hunt point toward a hidden medallion and a $2,000 prize. Celebrated since 1985, Winterfest draws 100,000 brave souls out into the cold.

updowntowners.com

# CONSIDER YOURSELF IRISH
## ON GREEN BEER SUNDAY

Syracuse takes St. Patrick's Day seriously—so seriously, locals start observing on the last Sunday in February. Green Beer Sunday, a Tipperary Hill tradition, was established in the 1960s by Coleman's Authentic Irish Pub owner Peter Coleman. At noon, one of the world's shortest parades begins under the famous upside-down stoplight at Tompkins and Milton. Bagpipers, Irish dancers, and the Grand Marshal march down to the pub a block and a half away where a tanker carrying green beer—allegedly from the Emerald Isle—is tapped; the Grand Marshal tastes the first draw. Festivities continue inside the pub and outside in Tipperary Square—the pub's parking lot—where Coleman's Pavilion hosts live music. No matter your heritage, everyone's Irish on this day.

Parade, intersection of Tompkins St. and Milton Ave.

Coleman's Authentic Irish Pub
100 S. Lowell Ave., 315-476-1933
colemansirishpub.com

# TIP

Don't like beer? Coleman's also serves
Hard Green Cider from 1911 Established
and the Loaded Leprechaun: a cocktail made
with 1911 Established Cold Brew Coffee
Vodka and Byrne Dairy's seasonal Mint Milk.
Available through St. Patrick's Day.

Green Hard Cider and Cold Brew Coffee Vodka
1911 Established, 1911established.com

Byrne Dairy Mint Milk
(late February through mid March)
byrnedairy.com/mint-milk

# APPLAUD
# THE ARTS WARMLY
## AT REDHOUSE

Redhouse Arts Center is a Syracuse success story. Established in
a narrow three-story building, its original theater seated less than
90; today in a new location, Redhouse—at 40,000 square feet—
has more than tripled in size. The smallest of its three theaters is
still bigger than the original, and the largest one fills its 350 seats
with world-class and family-friendly plays and musicals featuring
performers from across the country. A professional, not-for-profit
theater, Redhouse raised $10 million to renovate the former
Sibley's Department Store into the current multi-use event space.
With an attached garage and elevators, patrons can park, enter the
Center, see theater shows, live music, comedy, and other events,
and never set foot outside: a plus in snowy Syracuse.

400 S. Salina St., 315-362-2785
theredhouse.org

### TIP
The original Redhouse—the skinny red brick building that inspired
the name and logo—is now the home of Wunderbar. Visit Redhouse's
first location at 201 S. West St. and peek into the old theater to get a
sense of how this arts center has grown and flourished.

# FEEL *WILKOMMEN*
## AT INCLUSIVE WUNDERBAR

To the west of Armory Square, this bar/black box theater occupies the original Redhouse Arts Center building; its punny name is German for "wonderful." The bar half is inspired by the aesthetic of 1920s-1930s Berlin; the theater half is a dance hall, concert venue, and performance space for plays, burlesque, cabaret, and drag. In its own words, Wunderbar is "a safe space for queer people to be themselves," and everyone is welcome. Zero Proof Nights—for those who want to be sober and social— feature mocktails and kombucha on tap. Thursday is Trivia to Save Us All. Partnering with Breadcrumbs Productions, a non-profit professional theater and creative production company, they sponsor Artist Socials, networking for local creatives. Clearly Wunderbar lives up to its name.

201 S. West St., 315-671-0648
wunderbarsyr.com

Breadcrumbs Productions
breadcrumbsproductions.com

# KEEP IT REEL
## AT THE SYRACUSE
## INTERNATIONAL FILM FESTIVAL

Got a cinematographer's eye? Think you can spot the next great director or screenwriter? Since 2003, SIFF—the Syracuse International Film Festival—has showcased films that might not otherwise reach the general public. In early October, this multi-day festival screens dozens of shorts, features, and documentaries—submitted by filmmakers from over 20 countries—at venues throughout the city. Founded by Syracuse University film professor Owen Shapiro and his wife, Christine Fawcett-Shapiro, SIFF highlights local, independent, and international films, and has spotlighted indigenous filmmakers and films on disability in their lineup. Filmmaking competitions for college and high school students and a directors' roundtable with industry professionals sharing their experiences round out the programming. Purchase single-event tickets or an all-festival access pass for your Syracuse red carpet moment.

syracusefilmfest.com

# HARVEST HAPPY MEMORIES
## AT CRITZ FARMS

Navigate the Corn Maze. Ride the Cow Train. While fall is the busiest time of year, this family-owned farm sows fun in every season. For the kids: farm animals, Slide Mountain, and Kiddie Corral with a pirate ship and wooden train. For all ages: nature trails, farm tours, wagon rides, U-pick blueberries, apples, pumpkins, and Christmas trees. For adults: the Tasting Room with handcrafted hard ciders and ales, Critz Café, and Balsam Barn gift shop. Most activities are free year-round. Because it's so popular, the Fall Harvest Celebration (mid-September to end of October) is a ticketed event including all activities plus the Corn Maze and Cow Train. From the first sign of sap flowing in the sugarbush to the last cut evergreen bough, Critz is a family tradition.

3233 Rippleton Rd. (Rte. 13-S), Cazenovia, 315-662-3355
critzfarms.com

# JAM AT THESE JUMPIN' JOINTS
## FOR LIVE MUSIC

Syracuse bars sizzle—dozens of venues feature local performers, open mic events, and entertainment most nights of the week. Start with these four: two longtime stalwarts and two newer venues.

### Shifty's

A granddaddy at five decades with live music five nights a week, it's a hole in the wall, but everybody who's anybody has been to Shifty's.
1401 Burnet Ave., 315-474-0048
shiftysbar.com

### Funk & Waffles

Mondays are Dead Night, Thursdays through Saturdays are advance-sale ticketed concerts. Waffle-wise, they've been featured on Food Network's *Diners, Drive-Ins and Dives* after 15 years perfecting their art.
307 S. Clinton St., 315-474-1060
funknwaffles.com

### The 443 Social Club & Lounge

Focusing on live original acoustic music, they host regional and national singer-songwriters in a cozy, intimate atmosphere that attracts an older crowd. Sit outside for a tropical-vacation vibe.
443 Burnet Ave., 315-308-1386
443socialclub.com

### Jus Sum Jazz Lounge

Authentic Southern-style food and Soul Food Sundays share the spotlight with local live performers and DJs. Musical genres cover old school to more modern interpretations of jazz and other styles.
1965 W. Fayette St., 315-488-4540
jussumjazzlounge.com

# SPORTS
# AND RECREATION

# FOLLOW WHERE MULES ONCE TROD
## ALONG THE ERIE CANAL

Bike, walk, or run for miles along the best-known canal in the US. (Be thankful you're not pulling a boat.) Though this historic waterway is no longer continuous through Syracuse, the remaining portions are essential to our daily recreational life. To the west, Camillus Erie Canal Park has a two-mile seasonal canal boat tour; restored aqueduct; and the Sims Store Museum, a recreated canal store. To the east, the trailhead of the 36-mile Old Erie Canal State Park is on Butternut Drive; the first paved mile is largely treeless but an easy walk. Park at Cedar Bay or Burdick for a shadier stroll. Twelve miles east, Chittenango Landing Canal Boat Museum features a blacksmith shop and sawmill, canoe launch, restrooms, gift shop, and bike rentals during gift-shop business hours.

Camillus Erie Canal Park
5750 Devoe Rd., Camillus
315-488-3409
eriecanalcamillus.com

Old Erie Canal State Park
5628 Butternut Dr., East Syracuse
eriecanal.org/OECSHP.html

Cedar Bay and Burdick parking
cnyhiking.com/NYSP-OldErie
CanalButternutDrive.htm

Chittenango Landing
Canal Boat Museum
717 Lakeport Rd., Chittenango
315-687-3801, chittenangolanding.org

Erie Canal overview
nycanalmap.com

## TIP

After all that exercise, treat yourself to a meal at Wegmans, a supermarket with a cult following (see #83). The Old Erie Canal trailhead is right across from Butternut Creek Recreation and Nature Area—walk or drive over. From the Kinne Road parking lot, it's 0.7 miles along a wooded path to the Wegmans parking lot on Genesee Street in Dewitt.

6836 Kinne Rd., Fayetteville
cnyhiking.com/ButternutCreekRecreationalArea.htm

# DROP "CARRIER"
## AND JUST CALL IT THE DOME

This massive pre-cast concrete stadium is synonymous with Syracuse University; SU's basketball, football, and lacrosse teams play here. Dominating the skyline with its white fiberglass-fabric roof—its newly added exterior steel frame resembling a gentle roller coaster—it's the largest domed stadium in the Northeast and on any US college campus. And that makes sense in a city where snowfall has been recorded as early as October 1 and as late as May 17. The structure formerly known as the Carrier Dome is also a mega-concert venue, selling out shows performed by rock royalty including the Stones, The Who, Springsteen, the Dead, Bowie, Prince, and Elton John. With seating for 49,250, when The Dome crowd gets worked up, it earns its nickname, "The Loud House."

900 Irving Ave., 315-443-2121
carrierdome.com

# WALK ON
# (WHAT ONCE WAS)
## WATER AT CLINTON SQUARE

It's twice as nice at Syracuse's public square and plaza where fountains dance in summer and skaters spin in winter. Clinton Square has gone through many changes, but a 2011 renovation reimagined the old Erie Canal site as a modern urban oasis. Today, its mirror-like expanse returns a welcome body of water—albeit shallow—to the heart of the city. In summer, the Downtown Farmers Market is held here on Tuesdays, and on festival weekends, the water is drained and white tents roost in the plaza like a flock of seagulls. In winter, Clinton Square becomes a public skating rink offering rentals and is home to the city's Christmas Tree and annual Tree Lighting in November. In every season, the self-guided Downtown Walking Tour begins here.

161 W. Genesee St., 315-423-0219
syracuse.ny.us/Parks/clintonSquareEvents.html

Winter Ice Rink
skatesinthecity.com

November Tree Lighting
syracusetreelighting.com

# STROLL ONONDAGA LAKE PARK, THE "CENTRAL PARK OF CNY"

Stand under the leafy canopy of its wooded shores, look out over its sun-struck waters, and you won't believe Onondaga Lake is Syracuse's most extreme makeover story. Today, seven miles of parklands and paths are popular with walkers, runners, cyclists, rollerbladers, dog owners, fishermen, and picnickers. The East Shore Trail begins by the playground/skatepark and runs past the Salt Museum, boat launch, seasonal bathrooms, and over Long Branch Road Bridge. The West Shore Trail connects the Lakeview Amphitheater and NYS Fairgrounds Orange Lot. There, a high bluff offers gorgeous views. In summer, visit the Salt Museum detailing the city's briny history. Sixty years ago, Onondaga Lake was called the most polluted lake in America after a century of toxic dumping. A lengthy cleanup reclaimed this sparkling blue gem.

106 Lake Dr., Liverpool, 315-451-7275
onondagacountyparks.com/parks/onondaga-lake-park

Park Map
onondagacountyparks.com/assets/Uploads/Onondaga-Lake-Park/
OLPmap2018color.pdf

## TIP

From April to mid-October,
Cuse Cycle rents two- and three-wheeled
bicycles, three- and five-seater surrey
quadricycles, inline skates, and bocce balls and
shuffleboard equipment. They're next to the
Griffin Visitor Center.

6770 Onondaga Lake Pkwy., Liverpool, 315-453-6718
onondagacountyparks.com/activity/rentals-bikes-and-skates
cusecyclerentals.com

# SWEAR YOU'RE IN THE CARIBBEAN
## AT GREEN LAKES

Look but don't disturb the vibrant turquoise-blue water. Although swimming and boating are permitted at this NYS park/campground, the prettiest spots are protected and posted with "Do Not Enter Water" signs. Green Lake and its sister Round Lake are an intense, unbelievable color because they're rare meromictic lakes. Surface and lower waters never mix; thus, the bottom layers of sediment hold information on ancient plant and animal life. Green Lake was the first lake in North America classified as meromictic; it's been continually studied since 1839. Swimming and boating are restricted to the shallow northeast end; since the lake deepens to 195 feet, even wading is off-limits. Walk the easy two-mile Green Lake trail for the views. The Round Lake trail adds another .95 mile and is much less traveled.

7900 Green Lakes Rd., Fayetteville, 315-637-6111
parks.ny.gov/parks/greenlakes

# PLAY ALL DAY
## AT THE ENTERTAINMENT VENUES OF DESTINY USA

Explore, giggle, be a kid again—whatever your age, you'll find fun at the mall. Little ones love Billy Beez's tunnels, swings, slides, tubes, and sports courts. Apex Entertainment has bowling with full-menu lane service, a 50-game redemption arcade, bumper cars, laser tag, an X-Rider virtual reality thrill ride, axe throwing, and Hologate, a virtual gaming system. At RPM Raceway, drive an Italian-made go-kart around a European-style track up to 50 mph. At 5 Wits, immerse yourself in a live-action puzzle-solving experience. Inside WonderWorks, lie on a bed of nails or try out a hundred other interactive exhibits. Solve the Amazing Mirror Maze and end with a ride on the mall's ADA accessible antique carousel. It's your Destiny to have fun!

Billy Beez
315-701-5099
billybeezus.com/location/destiny-usa

Apex Entertainment
315-515-8666
apexentertainment.com/syracuse

RPM Raceway
315-423-7333
rpmraceway.com/syracuse-ny

5 Wits
315-988-4011, 5-wits.com/syracuse

WonderWorks
315-466-7700
wonderworksonline.com/destiny

Amazing Mirror Maze
315-476-2000, destinyusa.com/
tenants/amazing-mirror-maze

Antique Carousel
Food Court

● ● ● ● ● ● ● ● ● ● ● ● ● ● ● ● ● ● ● ● ● ● ● ●

# FLOCK TO THE MALL
## TO VIEW BALD EAGLES

Why does America's national bird hang out next to a mall parking lot? According to an Audubon official, New York State's top urban winter bald eagle roost is the wooded area behind Destiny USA, where Onondaga Creek flows into Onondaga Lake. Warm water is released by a nearby sewage treatment plant (you can't make this stuff up), attracting schools of gizzard shad and other fish. The steady flow and warm temperatures ensure an open patch of water for the eagles to hunt and fish. Just pull into the rear parking lot of Destiny to see them roosting in the trees. Best viewing: January-March between 7-9 a.m. and 4-5 p.m. Up to 50 have been spotted in one day. Follow Onondaga Audubon's Facebook page for details and photos.

9090 Destiny USA Dr. (south rear parking lot)
315-466-6000, destinyusa.com/eagles

Bald Eagles of Onondaga Lake
facebook.com/groups/baldeaglesofonondagalake

---

### TIP
If you're up for a cold winter walk, another good viewing spot is the pedestrian bridge at the southern end of the West Shore Trail. Park at the Honeywell Onondaga Lake Visitors Center or farther down at a smaller lot, then walk down to the bridge, which runs over the railroad tracks.

208 Restoration Way, 315-552-975
lakecleanup.com/public-engagement/onondaga-lake-visitors-center

---

# GET LIT ON A COLD WINTER'S NIGHT
## AT LIGHTS ON THE LAKE

During the holidays, do you search out neighborhoods where homeowners try to outshine each other with Christmas displays? Then you'll love this glowing drive-thru holiday extravaganza. From mid-November through early January, the East Shore Recreation Trail at Onondaga Lake Park transforms into Lights on the Lake. This two-mile stretch of night-time light displays includes the Land of Oz, a twinkling fantasy forest, an enchanted castle, and more. There's nothing high-tech here, just old-fashioned holiday fun—300 light displays that have become a Central New York tradition over the past thirty years. Local station Sunny 102.1 FM even broadcasts a dedicated holiday music channel as the soundtrack to your visit. Over 40,000 vehicles make the slow crawl through the trail each year. Drive, view, and be merry!

6751 Onondaga Lake Pkwy., Liverpool, 315-453-6712
lightsonthelake.com

---

### TIP
Buy your tickets online—none are available at the gate, and you have to pick your admission date in advance. Aim for Mondays or Tuesdays, the least expensive nights; on Fridays, Saturdays, and Sundays, prices triple. It's a flat rate no matter how many are in your vehicle, so pack 'em in.

---

# HEAR THE THUNDER
## OF CASCADING WATERFALLS

Take a hike that ends at a waterfall. When a stream meets a precipice, the steady force of falling water carves out places of magic. Here's a variety of choices.

## TIP

It's best to visit Tinkers Falls and Three Falls Woods in the spring when snowmelt boosts the water levels. Often by mid-summer, these waterfalls drop down to a trickle—and even disappear when it's dry. Both have limited trailhead parking that fills quickly.

### Chittenango Falls State Park
View the 167-foot waterfalls from top or bottom—trails lead to both.
2300 Rathbun Rd., Cazenovia, 315-492-1756
parks.ny.gov/parks/chittenangofalls

### Pratt's Falls County Park
This ribbon cascade has a 137-foot drop. The hike is steep in spots, but the overlook is worth the short jaunt.
7671 Pratt's Falls Rd., Manlius, 315-683-5550
onondagacountyparks.com/parks/pratts-falls-park

### Tinkers Falls
Choose between ease and adventure: the quarter-mile trail to the 50-foot falls is wide and relatively flat but scramble up farther to go behind the screen of water. It's located in the Labrador Unique Area where there are many more trails worth exploring.
Rte. 91, Tully (look for trailhead sign)
dec.ny.gov/lands/37070.html

### Three Falls Woods
A network of dirt paths reveals natural amphitheaters of rock and water perfect for wading.
4618 Sweet Rd., Manlius (look for CNY Land Trust trailhead), 315-575-8839
cnylandtrust.org/preserve/three-falls-woods

# SCORE A HOME RUN OF FUN
## AT A SYRACUSE METS GAME

Regardless of who's on the mound, every game starts with energetic pitching from General Manager Jason Smorol promising "the most amazing show on dirt!" This Minor League baseball team, a Triple-A affiliate of the New York Mets, plays at newly renovated NBT Bank Stadium, "the Disney of the North Side," where "nobody does affordable family fun like your Syracuse Mets!" And Smorol's non-stop promotions, giveaways, and special deals draw crowds. Dollar Thursdays feature $1 hot dogs and beverages, $2 beers and 1911 hard ciders. On Family Sunday Kids Eat Free: children 12 and under get a hot dog, drink, popcorn, and ice cream. Enjoy Taco Tuesdays, Craft Beer Fridays, Bark at the Park dog-friendly games, T-shirt and bobblehead giveaways, and fireworks. Summer is the Syracuse Mets.

NBT Bank Stadium
1 Tex Simone Dr., 315-474-7833
milb.com/syracuse

# STEP OUTSIDE YOUR COMFORT ZONE
## AT CANYON CLIMB ADVENTURE

Reach new heights, even if you're afraid of falling. Inside Destiny USA is the world's largest suspended indoor ropes course. Canyon Climb hangs 70 feet above the mall floor, encompasses three levels, and challenges you with 81 different obstacles to knock you off balance. But don't worry: a secure harness and thick safety rope ensure that you won't fall—you'll just dangle. Walk a tightrope, step between wobbly wooden rungs, clutch on to something, anything! Take a break on the sturdy metal platforms affixed to the mall's structural columns and quiet those quaking knees. During the day, the course—well-lit under the mall's glass ceiling—is easier to see (both good and bad). At night, colored spotlights are atmospheric—and dimmer. All the better to hide your fears. You can do it!

WonderWorks, Destiny USA
2 Destiny Dr., 315-466-7700
wonderworksonline.com/destiny/the-experience/canyon-climb

# LEARN WHY CONSERVATION MATTERS
## AT THE ROSAMOND GIFFORD ZOO

Pandas and penguins and bears, oh my! The Rosamond Gifford Zoo at Burnet Park monitors the conservation status of these species, so new babies born to the red pandas (endangered), Humboldt penguins (vulnerable) and the arrival of a young Andean bear (vulnerable), are enthusiastically celebrated. Both indoor and outdoor habitats are home to 700 animals representing 216 species. The main environmental "green building" houses the aquarium: see a Giant Pacific octopus and an ocean reef with tropical fish. A free-flight aviary reproduces a tropical rainforest environment. The outdoor Wildlife Trail traverses the Asian Elephant Preserve, Penguin Coast, and Primate Park. The zoo's emphasis on conservation and breeding places it among the top 10 percent of zoos in North America earning accreditation by the Association of Zoos and Aquariums.

1 Conservation Pl., 315-435-8511
rosamondgiffordzoo.org

## TIP

Annual events cater to both kids and adults. Zoo Boo is a "kooky not spooky" daytime Halloween celebration; wear costumes, chat with zookeepers, and trick or treat. During the summer, Brew at the Zoo brings close to fifty breweries and wineries in for a fundraiser with food trucks and live music.

# SEEK SERENITY
## IN UPPER ONONDAGA PARK

Visit this unexpectedly romantic city park and step through a portal in time. A lovely 15-acre lake is surrounded by verdant lawns and forested slopes; at the southern end a small island topped with a picturesque gazebo is accessible by a wooden footbridge. Nearby, a larger stone bridge is surrounded by weeping willows, and in summer a pair of fountains ripple the lake's quiet surface. The landscape has a manicured feel, and in fact it's man-made; Hiawatha Lake was developed from what was once the old Wilkinson reservoir built to provide city water. The 67-acre park is in the hilltop Strathmore neighborhood; walk along its western border—and ogle the stately brick and Tudor-style homes lining Onondaga Lake Drive—for a postcard-perfect photo.

500 Summit Ave., 315-473-4330
syracuse.ny.us/Parks/onondagaParkUpper.html

---

### TIP
Enjoy an uninterrupted view of University Hill and downtown Syracuse near the eastern edge of Upper Onondaga Park. The ideal spot is at the Mountain Goat Run monument on Little Round Top.

# REV UP YOUR ENGINE
## AT THE SYRACUSE NATIONALS

With live music and food, it's like the New York State Fair minus farm animals, and the only rides are cars. In mid-July, the Fairgrounds hosts the Northeast's largest car show: 8,000 classic cars, 400 vendors, 90,000 enthusiasts. Visit Memories on Main Street for vintage and classic cars. The Syracuse Signature Showcase features new muscle cars, trucks, and high-end unique show vehicles. Sparky's Rockabilly Roundup is retro cool with Rat Rods—rusty, deliberately worn-looking custom cars—and the biggest Pin-Up Girl contest in the Northeast. Watch artists at work in the Charity Brush Bash, pinstriping and airbrushing vehicles to benefit the Ronald McDonald House. American Muscle Sunday brings out Camaros, Mustangs, Chargers, and Corvettes, while the Syracuse Mini-Nationals is a model car show.

NY State Fairgrounds
syracusenationals.com

# BLISS OUT
## AT BALTIMORE WOODS AND SYCAMORE HILL GARDENS

The draw of this nature center in Marcellus is its focus on environmental education and stewardship—and an incredible once-a-year event. Owned by the Central New York Land Trust, 182-acre Baltimore Woods is overseen by conservationists and other professionals who put "nature in your hands" through programs for children and adults. Each year they partner with Sycamore Hill Gardens, which opens for just one day— Mother's Day—for a not-to-be-missed benefit event. Take your time wandering the garden's 30+ acres. A small lake with a soaring fountain, a Japanese-style bridge, hidden statues, gongs and bells, a massive hedge maze, and stone towers sit among blossoming trees and flowers. It's CNY's most astonishing and magical landscape. For tickets, check the website in early spring.

4007 Bishop Hill Rd., Marcellus, 315-673-1350
baltimorewoods.org

Sycamore Hill Gardens
sycamorehillgardens.com

# BREAK THE ICE WITH FANS
## AT A SYRACUSE CRUNCH GAME

Enthusiastic crowds make winter wild at Crunch games, cheering on players who frequently advance to the NHL. This professional ice hockey team, affiliated with the NHL's Tampa Bay Lightning, is part of the American Hockey League. At every home game at the War Memorial, the energy is high, the music loud, the lights flashing, and the kiss cam sometimes a little embarrassing. Fans who want to get involved can join the Blink Fitness Crunch Crew, a promotional team helping with game day events and outside community activities. Kids can join the Crunch Bunch; a one-time fee gets you special merchandise items, exclusive nights, and a post-game skate. Even dogs are welcomed—Pucks for Paws brings canines to the rink, with proceeds benefitting animal welfare programs.

Upstate Medical University Arena at the Onondaga County War Memorial
800 S. State St., 315-473-4444
syracusecrunch.com

# ROCK AROUND THE LAKE
## AT CLARK RESERVATION

Two miles from the city limits, discover a slice of the Adirondack Mountains—well, at least it feels that way. Just south of Syracuse, this half-circle of rugged limestone cliffs surrounding a glacial lake is "a geologic wonder of the last ice age and a botanist's paradise" according to Clark Reservation's website. For a short visit, the relatively flat mile-long Mildred Faust Trail is the easiest: a quick walk through forests, ferns, and mosses. For a more strenuous hike, try Cliff Trail along the rim, or Table Rock Trail furrowed by deep clefts. Want a solid workout? Take the stairs down to the lake; heading back up, your quads will curse. Scramble over rocky outcroppings, but stay safe—it's a 180-foot drop from cliffside to water's edge.

6105 E. Seneca Tpke., Jamesville, 315-492-1756
parks.ny.gov/parks/clarkreservation

# PUTTER
# AN AFTERNOON AWAY
## AT FAIRMOUNT GLEN MINIATURE GOLF

In a pocket-sized valley just up the hill from a busy Target lies this frozen-in-time attraction. Eighteen holes are overhung by tall trees and lush with grasses, flowers, and plantings. Play amidst the splash of fountains, waterfalls, and a babbling brook crossed by a covered bridge. It's not flashy—it's old-fashioned mini-golf where you putt through traditional layouts like the windmill, red barn, castle, and pinball machine. The game ends just like every classic miniature golf course—with a final putt into the clown's face, fenced off to prevent cheating. Get your ball in the nose for a free game—it's much harder than it looks. A summertime destination in CNY for over seven decades, Fairmount Glen is quaint, nostalgic, and a generational favorite.

210 Onondaga Rd., 315-487-0546
fairmountglen.com

# TRY SOMETHING NEW
## AT ONONDAGA COUNTY PARKS

At least one of Onondaga County's parks offers something you've always wanted to try. At Jamesville Beach, you can swim in Jamesville Reservoir, play disc golf, or let Rover run at the dog park. At Beaver Lake, you can canoe, kayak, cross-country ski, snowshoe, or take up bird-watching in their 100 Bird Challenge to win a T-shirt proclaiming "I Saw-whet at Beaver Lake, 100 birds." At Highland Forest, book horseback riding, a horse-drawn sleigh- or hay-ride, go mountain biking or sledding, or rent snowshoes or cross-country skis. At Carpenter's Brook, feed the fish, volunteer to stock trout, or sign up for a seasonal fishing program—family, senior, and special-needs friendly. And you thought you'd done it all . . .

Jamesville Beach Park
3992 Apulia Rd., Jamesville, 315-435-5252
onondagacountyparks.com/parks/jamesville-beach-park

Beaver Lake Nature Center
8477 E. Mud Lake Rd., Baldwinsville, 315-638-2519
onondagacountyparks.com/parks/beaver-lake-nature-center

Highland Forest
1254 Highland Park Rd., Fabius, 315-683-5550
onondagacountyparks.com/parks/highland-forest

Carpenter's Brook Fish Hatchery
1672 Rte. 321, Elbridge, 315-689-9367
onondagacountyparks.com/parks/carpenters-brook-fish-hatchery

## TIP

Beaver Lake Nature Center hosts two popular events each fall. The Golden Harvest Festival in mid-September is an old-fashioned country fair–style event with crafts, live music, a living scarecrow, and pie-eating contests. In October, hundreds of carved jack-o-lanterns light up the night at Enchanted Beaver Lake, an event which sells out quickly. Stay up to date on their Facebook page.

facebook.com/beaverlakenaturecenter

# CULTURE AND HISTORY

# BECOME A SYRACUSE WISE GUY
## AT THE OHA

Admittedly, it's not a sexy name: Onondaga Historical Association. But a visit to what's essentially the Museum of Syracuse is like buying Apple stock in 1980—an incredible value. Out-of-towners, you'll get a crash course in Syracuse 101 and pass for a local as you name-drop Syracuse China and *The Magic Toy Shop*—a beloved children's TV show that ran for 27 years. Syracuse natives, you'll grow nostalgic over reminders of the old days—Congress beer, Economy Bookstore, downtown department stores Sibley's, Dey Brothers, The Addis Company, and—coolest of all—the children's monorail that circled the toy department at E. W. Edwards. And just like at Disney, you'll exit through the gift shop where books on local lore and Central New York–themed items make great souvenirs.

321 Montgomery St., 315-428-1864
cnyhistory.org

---

### TIP
Be sure to see *Freedom Bound: Syracuse and the Underground Railroad*, a life-sized diorama with music and voices illustrating the city's role in the abolition movement. Ask in the gift shop and they'll start the 15-minute show when you're ready.

---

# SEE GREEN
## AT THE UPSIDE-DOWN TRAFFIC LIGHT

It's allegedly the only green-over-red stoplight in the world, reversing the usual order. Located in Syracuse's Tipperary Hill neighborhood, the traffic light at the intersection of Tompkins and Milton celebrates Irish pride and persistence. The story goes that when the light was installed, Irish youth hated British red dominating Irish green, so they smashed the top lens with a well-aimed stone. After each repair, the stone throwers broke it again. Finally, city officials made the green-on-top permanent. In 1997, the Stone Throwers statue depicting an Irish immigrant family—father gesturing toward the light to his wife, son, and daughter—was erected on the corner. Each year at 12:01 am on St. Patrick's Day, Irish celebrants paint a large green shamrock under the light.

Intersection of Tompkins St. and Milton Ave.

Stone Throwers Park (Tipperary Hill Heritage Memorial)
northeast corner of Tompkins and Milton
syracuse.ny.us/Parks/StoneThrowersPark.html

# ADMIRE AMERICAN ART
## AT THE EVERSON MUSEUM

Twenty years before Parisians flocked to the Louvre for the opening of its glass Pyramid in 1988, internationally acclaimed architect I.M. Pei had another notable opening—the Everson, his first museum design. Syracuse's art museum also shares bloodlines with NYC's Metropolitan Museum of Art—George Fisk Comfort helped established both. The Everson has always been visionary. In 1911, it was the first museum to collect only American art, and now it holds pieces from colonial to contemporary. It also launched one of the country's first video art collections; today it's one of the world's largest. An initial 1916 investment in porcelain by Syracuse potter Adelaide Alsop Robineau has grown into one of the most comprehensive collections of American ceramic art. Most locals don't realize that our museum is world class.

401 Harrison St., 315-474-6064
everson.org

# TRAVEL BACK IN TIME
## WITH THE DOWNTOWN
## HISTORIC WALKING TOUR

It's the city's ultimate bargain: free, self-guided, and available on phone or tablet thanks to the Downtown Committee of Syracuse. Start at Clinton Square and tour 71 historic sites with photos, background info from the Onondaga Historical Association, and a detailed route map. Architecture buffs will spot examples of Neo-Classical, Art Deco, Greek Revival, Queen Anne, Victorian Gothic, Metropolitan, and Beaux Arts designs. In Armory Square, sports fans can take selfies under a replica of the NBA's 24-second shot clock, which, according to the OHA, "was first used in Syracuse in 1954 and is credited with changing basketball and saving the National Basketball Association." If you lose your way en route, press the I'M LOST button to get back on track. Even locals will enjoy this comprehensive tour.

Historic Walking Tour
315-422-8284, downtownsyracuse.com/downtown-guides

---

### TIP

Do not miss #3, the Niagara Mohawk Building (now owned by National Grid), a stunning example of Art Deco architecture. Its aluminum, black glass, and stainless-steel facade is dominated by, a winged statue over the main entrance. At night, lit by colored lights reflecting the season and special events, the building is breathtaking.

300 Erie Blvd. W., nps.gov/articles/niagara-hudson-building-ny.htm

---

# PRACTICE GRATITUDE
## AT SKÄ•NOÑH, THE GREAT LAW OF PEACE CENTER

"Onondaga" comes from the area's original inhabitants—the People of the Hills—one of five nations that came together as the Haudenosaunee, the People of the Longhouse. At the spiritual and political center, the Onondagas served as keepers of the Central Fire. At Skä•noñh (an Onondaga greeting meaning "Peace and Wellness") exhibits tell of this coming together in 1,000 A.D. One of world's oldest participatory democracies, the Haudenosaunee influenced the Founding Fathers who framed the US Constitution. Learn why gratitude and thanks are central to this thousand-year-old tradition. Outside, a re-created French mission settled by the Jesuits illustrates life in the 17th century. Part of the Onondaga Historical Association, Skä•noñh is a Haudenosaunee Heritage Center, presenting history through the lens of the Onondaga Nation.

6680 Onondaga Lake Pkwy., Liverpool, 315-453-6767
skanonhcenter.org and cnyhistory.org/visit/skanonh

# REVISIT AMERICA'S HISTORIC WATERWAY
## AT THE ERIE CANAL MUSEUM

Back before interstate highways, bargemen and women—intrepid individuals similar to today's truck drivers transporting cargo long distance—were the backbone of commerce. In the same way highways use weigh stations to measure the weight of tractor-trailers, a weighlock weighed canal boats, levying a toll to use the Erie Canal. The last remaining weighlock is the home of the Erie Canal Museum. Inside the 1850 Weighlock Building you'll learn about 'Clinton's Ditch,' the engineering marvel—envisioned by NYS governor Dewitt Clinton—that became world-famous. Walk through a full-size canal boat replica. Experience life in a canal town including a canal-era tavern, general store, and theater. See what folks ate, drank, and wore. It's time travel: entertaining, educational, and essential to understanding Syracuse's history.

318 Erie Blvd. E., 315-471-0593
eriecanalmuseum.org

# PLAY OUT YOUR PERIOD DRAMA
## AT LORENZO STATE HISTORIC SITE

Fans of *Bridgerton* and *Downton Abbey* will appreciate this beautifully restored ancestral lakeside home of Dutch land agent John Lincklaen, who founded the village of Cazenovia in 1793 and built Lorenzo in 1807. Travel to the 1800s as you walk through high-ceilinged rooms decorated with original furnishings, including a crystal- and china-laden dining table set for a formal meal. Two lake-view bedrooms and a collection of Hudson River School landscape paintings are especially appealing. Plus, a look at of those who served shows the upstairs/downstairs disparity with honesty. You can visit the formal gardens, Dark Aisle Arboretum, and outbuildings for free; there's a nominal fee to tour the Federal-style house. Open late May through early October and for "Christmas at Lorenzo" and other seasonal events.

17 Rippleton Rd., Cazenovia, 315-655-3200
parks.ny.gov/historic-sites/lorenzo

# ASK WHERE THEY "GET THEIR IDEAS"
## AT THE GIFFORD AUTHOR SERIES

For over 25 years, world-famous writers like Margaret Atwood, Jonathan Franzen, Amy Tan, Neil Gaiman, John Irving, and 150 others have come to Syracuse to support our library system. It's the largest library-related lecture series in the country, run by FOCL—Friends of the Central Library. Ticket sales benefit library programs and services that strengthen the community. Instead of reading, authors share personal stories, discuss the inspiration behind their books, talk about writing craft, and answer audience-posed questions. It's intimate, lively, and insightful, and it's a bucket-list item for readers. Although we call ourselves the Salt City because of our briny history, S-A-L-T could also be an acronym for "Syracuse: America's Literary Town"—and the Gifford Author Series is an influential part of that legacy.

Friends of the Central Library
447 S. Salina St., 315-435-1832
foclsyracuse.org

# FEED YOUR BRAIN
## AT THE MOST

MOST is short for the Milton J. Rubenstein Museum of Science & Technology, but it's really a place for learning through play. Walk through an enormous beating heart and its chambers. Create mountains, valleys, and plains in an augmented reality sandbox. Touch dinosaur skin and teeth and see a lifelike moving dino mother her hatchlings. Sit in a cockpit mockup of an F-16 fighter jet. Marvel at Toothpick World, which holds two Guinness World Records; built by North Syracuse toothpick engineer Stan Munro, it's just glue—and around 5 million toothpicks. Visit the Rothschild Apothecary Shop, an authentic recreation of a 1900s-era pharmacy. Investigate the Science Playhouse, a giant indoor five-level playground. With a state-of-the-art digital theater and a planetarium, the MOST is intelligent fun by design.

500 S. Franklin St., 315-425-9068

most.org

# WAX ELOQUENT ON QUARTER-SAWN OAK
## AND ALL THINGS STICKLEY

A leading figure in the American Arts and Crafts movement of the early 1900s, Gustav Stickley emphasized beauty and fine workmanship in his furniture—a style now known as Mission. Stickley Furniture is still in business today in Manlius, and the original L & JG Stickley factory (owned by brothers Leopold and John George) houses the Stickley Museum. This 8,000-square-foot exhibit gallery contains furniture and accessories from the early days to today, displaying designs so enduring, Barbra Streisand, Brad Pitt, and Jack Nicholson are collectors. If seeing isn't enough, purchase new at the nearby Stickley furniture showroom or find original Stickley pieces at Dalton's. The Gustav Stickley House, occupied by Stickley on and off until his death in 1942, is under restoration; it'll open as a museum with overnight stays.

Stickley Museum
300 Orchard St. (second floor)
Fayetteville, stickleymuseum.com

Dalton's American Decorative Arts
1931 James St., 315-463-1568
daltons.com

Stickley Furniture
Towne Center Shopping Plaza
300 Towne Dr., Fayetteville
315-637-7770, shopstickley.com/
locations/fayetteville-ny

Gustav Stickley House
438 Columbus Ave.
gustavstickleyhousefoundation.org

# MAKE THE CITY YOUR OYSTER
## ATOP THE HOTEL SYRACUSE

Though the hotel has since been renovated, one room could display the plaque "John Lennon slept here." In 1971, he and Yoko Ono celebrated his 31st birthday playing with Ringo Starr and Eric Clapton. Get the details on this and other stories as you tour this grand hotel with Scott Peal of the Onondaga Historical Association. For 1/20th the price of an overnight stay, you'll walk through and marvel at the Presidential Suite, Persian Terrace, and the posh Bridal Rotunda. This local landmark first opened in 1924 and in 2016 was refurbished at a cost of $82 million. The views from the gilded Grand Ballroom, lit by chandeliers suspended from a cloud-strewn ceiling, are unparalleled. The tour is 90 minutes, but Scott occasionally goes longer for smaller groups.

Marriott Syracuse Downtown
100 E. Onondaga St., 315-474-2424
marriott.com/hotels/travel/syrmc-marriott-syracuse-downtown

Hotel Syracuse Tour
315-428-1864
cnyhistory.org/hotel-syracuse-tours

# CHANGE YOUR MIND
## AT ART GALLERIES
## AMPLIFYING DIVERSE VOICES

Art—whether it's two-dimensional or three-dimensional, static or active—has the ability to infiltrate and influence individuals and communities. Syracuse's dynamic multicultural resources include three galleries that flex to include live performances and events. The Community Folk Art Center celebrates and elevates artists of the African Diaspora and promotes cultural pluralism through exhibitions, film screenings, gallery talks, theater, and dance. Point of Contact showcases contemporary verbal and visual arts, with an emphasis on Latin American artists and writers. Despite its name, ArtRage is open and embracing, a social justice arts organization dedicated to breaking down the art world's boundaries and welcoming all with the belief that everyone has the right to art. Their PosterWorks gift shop stocks over 100 images—find your statement piece there.

Community Folk Art Center
805 E. Genesee St.
315-442-2230
communityfolkartcenter.org

Punto de Contacto/
Point of Contact Gallery
350 W. Fayette St., 314-443-2169
puntopoint.org

ArtRage, the Norton Putter Gallery
505 Hawley Ave., 315-218-5711
artragegallery.org

# TRACE THE UNDERGROUND RAILROAD
## THROUGH SYRACUSE'S FREEDOM TRAIL

An example of unity across cultural divides, the Underground Railroad involved both rich and poor, black and white, all risking their lives to liberate enslaved people. From grand mansions and architecturally notable buildings to humble two-story houses, the Underground Railroad can be traced through a dozen sites in Syracuse thanks to the Preservation Association of CNY. Ironically, several now house restaurants, and though they don't focus on local history, you can dine in them, knowing their cultural significance. These locations include the Courier Building, the Dana Block (where the law office of New York State's first Black attorney was located), and Wesleyan Methodist Church. The smaller private homes can't be toured, but the Mansion on James—home of the George and Rebecca Barnes Foundation—accommodates visitors; see their website.

Various city locations
pacny.net/freedom_trail (map, narrative, and photos)

The Mansion on James
930 James St., 315-422-2445
mansiononjames.com

## TIP

A source of local pride, the bronze Jerry Rescue sculpture commemorates an 1851 act of resistance. Opposing the newly enacted Fugitive Slave Act, white and black abolitionists broke into a police station to release William "Jerry" Henry, a 40-year-old enslaved man from Missouri, who reached freedom in Canada a few days later.

Clinton Square
161 W. Genesee St.
cnyhistory.org/2014/10/jerry-rescue

# CLIMB UNIVERSITY HILL
## FOR MUSIC, ART, AND ROSES

A Hogwarts-like castle. A museum housing 5,000 years of art. A Frankenstein tree of grafted branches. Roses blooming for days. Wonders abound on the Hill, home to Syracuse University. The building known as Crouse College—Syracuse's Hogwarts— houses SU's Setnor School of Music. Built in 1889, its 650-seat concert hall, soaring 70 feet to an open timber roof, hosts 200 free performances each year. Inside SU's Schaffer Art Building, the Art Museum boasts nearly 45,000 pieces in its permanent collection. The Tree of 40 Fruit, created by SU art professor Sam Van Aken, blooms pink and white and bears peaches, plums, apricots, nectarines, cherries, and almonds. Nearby, at Thornden Park's Mills Rose Garden, 3,000 bushes surround a picturesque gazebo. In full bloom in June, the sight is pure magic.

Setnor School of Music
150 Crouse Dr., 315-443-2191
vpa.syr.edu/academics/music/facilities

Art Museum, Shaffer Art Building
315-443-4097
museum.syr.edu

Tree of 40 Fruit
Shaw Quad outside Hinds Hall
syracuse.edu/stories/tree-of-40-
fruit-sam-van-aken

E.M. Mills Rose Garden
at Thornden Park
501 Ostrom Ave.
syracuserosesociety.org/
Mills-Rose-Garden.php

# WANDER THE GALLERY-WITHOUT-WALLS
## THAT IS STONE QUARRY HILL ART PARK

Ramble among the meadows, woods, hillsides, and ponds to discover and interact with large-scale sculptural art. Over fifty pieces await your exploration. Some pieces are meant to be touched and—in the case of *Earth Ear*, a giant ear erupting out of the ground—sat on. Left out in the elements, they weather; and for some, like *The Fall of Disco Mickey* (the iconic Mouse half buried and yet still smiling), it's part of the art. This "landscape of process" spreads out across 104 acres in distinct areas: Upper and Lower Meadow, East and Roadside Meadows, Picnic Hill, Hillside, Hilltop, Upper and Lower Exit Fields, Piney Woods, and The Secret Garden. Founded in 1991 by Dorothy and Robert Reister, it's open every day of the year—$5 donation suggested.

3883 Stone Quarry Hill Rd., Cazenovia
sqhap.org

# BOOK A TOUR OR GHOST WALK
## AT OAKWOOD CEMETERY

*Syracuse University Magazine* has called Oakwood "a Victorian park for the upstate New York elite." Right next to the SU campus, its 160 acres remain shadowy, romantic, and quiet—a favorite place for the university chancellor, professors, students, and the public to walk, run, or simply ramble. Dimpled with hills and valleys, the cemetery is an open-air museum filled with monuments, mausoleums, and funerary sculpture. Designed by landscape architect Howard Daniels in 1859, Oakwood's 1879 memorial chapel is the work of Joseph Lyman Silsbee, who once tutored an apprentice named Frank Lloyd Wright. The Historic Oakwood Cemetery Preservation Association (HOCPA) offers tours, most of which are free. The OHA—Onondaga Historical Association— hosts Ghosts Walks introducing "residents" of Oakwood who tell their stories; professional actors truly bring the dead back to life.

Oakwood Cemetery
940 Comstock Ave., 315-475-2194
oakwoodofsyracuse.com

Historic Oakwood Cemetery
Preservation Association (HOCPA)
315-415-2954
hocpa.org

Historic Ghostwalks at Oakwood
315-428-1864
cnyhistory.org/ghostwalk

## TIP

If you're a fan of Stickley furniture and have visited every other Stickley site, you can pay homage to Gustav Stickley (March 9, 1858–April 20, 1942)—the designer behind Mission-style furniture—at his final resting place, a simple and unassuming marker at section B 233.

# COUNT DOWN SUMMER
## AT CULTURAL FESTIVALS
## AT AREA CHURCHES

Syracuse's diverse houses of worship throw open their doors each summer with cultural festivals featuring food, music, dance, and fellowship. Together, these three have celebrated more than 200 years.

## St. Sophia's Greek Fest

Nearing its 50th year, this four-day event in early June is always packed. Volunteers make 15,000 pieces of baklava and 32,000 loukomades (honey puffs) and still run out. 325 Waring Rd., 315-446-5222 syracusegreekfest.com

## St. Elias Middle Eastern Festival

For 90 years, they've celebrated Arabic culture in early July. Members hand-roll 20,000 stuffed grape leaves; prepare falafel, beef or chicken schawarma, and gyro; and collaborate with Gannon's (see #17) to create pistachio, rose water, and orange blossom ice cream. 4988 Onondaga Rd. (Rt. 173), 315-399-7912 syracusemideastfest.com

## St. John the Baptist Ukrainian Festival

For eight decades, they've sold pyrohy (what Americans call pierogi), preparing over 13,500 for the 12,000 attendees at this two-day festival in late July. 207 Tompkins St., 315-478-5109 stjohnbaptistucc.com

# MEET THE MOTHER-IN-LAW OF OZ
## AT THE MATILDA JOSLYN GAGE HOUSE

A woman way ahead of her time, Gage was the ultimate influencer whom time has forgotten. An abolitionist, activist, and ardent feminist, she introduced *Wizard of Oz* author L. Frank Baum and suffragists Susan B. Anthony and Elizabeth Cady Stanton to ideas that changed history. Baum married Gage's daughter, Maud, and was guided by Gage's philosophy and beliefs. She studied the Haudenosaunee (Iroquois) and their family and governmental structures based on female authority. Using this model of Native women's rights, she introduced these concepts to her white suffragist sisters. Her work earned her honorary adoption into the Wolf Clan of the Mohawk Nation and the clan name "She Who Holds the Sky." Learn more about women's rights, Native American justice, the Underground Railroad, and her connection to Oz at this museum/center of the Gage Foundation.

210 E. Genesee St., Fayetteville, 315-637-9311
matildajoslyngage.org

# TIP

Matilda Joslyn Gage encouraged her son-in-law's literary aspirations, telling him, "Write down those stories you tell your sons!" L. Frank Baum, Maud, and their children lived in the Gage house during the summer of 1887. Today the house features the Family Parlor Oz Room—where Baum married Maud—and is the only home where Baum lived that is open to the public.

# GO WITH THE FLOW
## ALONG CREEKWALK

Connecting downtown with the lakefront near Destiny USA, this urban pedestrian route (mostly) follows Onondaga Creek as it meanders northwest through the city. The route is 2.6 miles long starting at the southern trailhead in Armory Square and ending at the Onondaga Lake shoreline. It's a true creekside stroll through Armory Square with public art along the marked route. At Washington Street the route swings away and follows city streets for nearly half a mile; stop and admire the iconic Art Deco NiMo building at Erie Boulevard. The route rejoins the creek at Wallace Street. The most attractive sections are at Franklin Square and at Kirkpatrick Street where the creek widens into the Inner Harbor. Download the Creekwalk map for more info; look for interpretive signage on points of interest.

syrgov.net/Creekwalk.aspx

Map
syrgov.net/uploadedFiles/Departments/
Planning_and_Sustainability/creekwalk_brochure.pdf

### TIP
With sections of Creekwalk passing through thick growth along undeveloped stretches, particularly north of Bear Street, the trail can feel isolated. Take precautions, and to stay absolutely safe, don't walk alone in these areas.

# FIND YOUR MUSE
## AT THE YMCA'S
## DOWNTOWN WRITERS CENTER

Don't wait for a presidential inauguration to discover the next Amanda Gorman. On Friday nights, free readings are sponsored by this community center for the literary arts. Located at the Downtown YMCA, the Downtown Writers Center brings established and emerging poets and writers to town for public readings—or hosts them on Zoom. They also offer creative writing workshops at all levels from beginner to pro, taught by professional writers. Classes in poetry, fiction, non-fiction, drama, screenwriting, and songwriting are in-person and online. For teen and tween writers, the Young Authors Academy meets on Saturdays. The DWC also celebrates the Syracuse writing community; each year local writers are fêted at the CNY Book Awards, with winners announced in various categories. If you've always wanted to write, start here.

340 Montgomery St., 315-474-6851
ymcacny.org/programs/arts/creative-writing

# PUT YOURSELF IN THE PICTURE
## WITH SYRACUSE STREET ART

Public art is a statement that individualizes a city; it's a postcard writ large. While Syracuse's public art is plentiful, these six murals reflect our unique story.

## TIP
As you drive around Syracuse, look for the eyes. Unlike the aforementioned commissioned art, these spray-painted eyeballs appear everywhere—illegally. Syracuse journalist Katrina Tulloch credits them to graffiti artist Vacant. Locations change, so keep your own eyes open.

### Clinton Serenade
Corky Goss and Chip Miller revisit the Erie Canal circa 1912 under the enchantment of moonlight.
126 N. Salina St.

### We Are the Mighty Salt City
Cayetano Valenzuela's elegant mix of typefaces celebrates our historical nickname.
420 E. Genesee St.

### Trolley
Robert D'Agostino's Erie Canal trolley appears 3-D with figures popping out of the brickwork.
208 N. Townsend St.

### Put the U Back in Syracuse
Two post-pandemic murals by Ally Walker were funded to encourage a return to restaurants and shopping. Made for selfies.
327 W. Fayette St. and 309 S. Warren St.

### You've Made It . . . & . . . Till Next Time
In these two adjacent murals, John Bocksell highlights the basketball Shot Clock, first used in Syracuse; the actual Shot Clock monument is around the corner.
321 W. Fayette St. (both sides of the building)

### A Love Letter to Syracuse
Painted on train trestles, Steve Powers interviewed Syracuse residents to come up with six "love letters," which have become famous in the worldwide art community.
201–220 S. West St., 365 S. West St.
122–400 W. Fayette St., vimeo.com/15438315

# SHOPPING AND FASHION

# BUY LOCAL, GIFT THOUGHTFUL
## AT SALT CITY ARTISANS

A Syracuse T-shirt is an easy purchase, as a gift for yourself or others. But for the same price or less, why not choose an item of lasting beauty—and support a local artist? In the leafy Hawley Green neighborhood, Salt City Artisans houses the work of 40 to 50 creatives, most from the immediate Syracuse area. Owners Jeremy Dottin-Reina and Rick Reina showcase pottery, woodworking, jewelry, glass, linens, knitted goods, and their own Syracuse Soapworks products. Their premium-quality handcrafted natural soaps and bath items sell themselves; the moment you walk in the shop, the smell is heavenly. An added bonus: they'll artfully package your purchase so it's suitable for gift-giving. Instead of a souvenir, come away with a memento—a gift anyone would truly treasure.

226 Hawley Ave., 315-479-0400
syracusesoapworks.com

## TIP
For under $5.00, their Erie Canal Soaps are like scented postcards, thick bars wrapped in vintage images of canal sites like Syracuse, Baldwinsville, and other upstate locales. One size fits all. Lather, rinse, repeat.

syracusesoapworks.com/products/erie-canal-soap-bars

# JOIN THE CULT-LIKE FANS
## OF WEGMANS GROCERY STORE

It's got a million followers on Twitter, Facebook, and Instagram. It's the subject of a high school musical. And for some job applicants, it's harder to get into than Harvard. With eight stores in the Syracuse area, we're used to Wegmans, the Disneyworld of supermarkets, but outsiders can't get enough. The produce section looks like a European open-air market. The sushi and pizza are fresh, and subs and sandwiches are made to order. In the Fairmount store, its prepared foods section mimics a fairytale village with lighted windows; take your meal to an ivy-twined second-floor balcony to people-watch. At 152,273 square feet, the Dewitt store has everything—gifts, housewares, high-end skincare—plus its Burger Bar restaurant serves beer. But really, any Wegmans is worth a visit.

3325 W. Genesee St., 315-487-1581 (Fairmount)

4722 Onondaga Blvd., 315-478-3313 (Onondaga)

4256 James St., 315-437-1534 (James St.)

7952 Brewerton Rd., Cicero, 315-698-6700 (Cicero)

6789 E. Genesee St., Fayetteville, 315-446-1180 (Dewitt)

4979 W. Taft Rd., Liverpool, 315-457-0514 (Taft Road)

7519 Oswego Rd., Liverpool, 315-546-1200 (John Glenn)

3955 Rte. 31, Liverpool, 315-622-4632 (Great Northern)

wegmans.com

# RALLY 'ROUND WOMEN-OWNED RETAIL
## IN MARCELLUS

In this picture-perfect country village, eclectic shops are run by women on second careers, juggling families, upcycling furniture, even working full-time. Just as Route 173W dips into the valley, the Wren's Den is a magic cottage amidst flowers and plants. Cards, gifts, and whimsical items are fetchingly displayed. In the village proper, vintage purveyor Marcellus Mercantile opens on weekends. Around the corner, AnnaBelle Design paints up a storm transforming furniture into fun pieces; she's also a jewelry-aholic. Close by, Olive + Fern is a hidden gem of contemporary goods with a boho aesthetic. A few miles southeast, a converted church is aptly named Rummage Heaven. There are three floors of antiques and repurposed furniture: sanctuary, choir loft, and basement. You'll need to set aside a whole day for shopping this unique area.

**The Wren's Den**
2756 W. Seneca Tpke., Marcellus
315-952-5954
thewrensden.business.site

**Marcellus Mercantile**
20 W. Main St., Marcellus
315-439-4197
facebook.com/marcellusmercantile1

**AnnaBelle Design Company**
19 North St., Marcellus, 315-569-2220
facebook.com/annabelledesigncompany

**Olive + Fern**
19 North St., Marcellus (behind Subway)
315-200-2464
facebook.com/shopolivefern

**Rummage Heaven**
3165 Amber Rd., Marcellus, 315-272-9236
facebook.com/rummageheaven

# TAKE THE STAIRS
## AT THE SYRACUSE ANTIQUE EXCHANGE

Wear a pedometer as you shop this five-story brick building with 20,000 square feet of retail space on four floors. Steps still count even when you don't notice the exercise. Over 70 dealers offer everything from architectural salvage and hardware to vintage clothing and jewelry. Antiques include Victorian and mid-century furniture, lighting, Art Deco pieces, clocks, sports memorabilia, wall art, books, china, glassware, and more. Their website features two convenient options: under SALES in the menu bar you can see current discounts offered by dealers in any of your favorite categories. Under TOUR, browse floor-by-floor with the 3D Tour feature; click on arrows to move between booths and click on the green link to inquire about specific items. The tour is updated every two weeks.

1629 N. Salina St., 315-471-1841
syracuseantiques.com

# BECOME A LOCAVORE
## AT THE CNY REGIONAL MARKET

The area's biggest farmers market is essentially a public market and food hall open from 7 a.m. until 2 p.m. every Saturday year-round. Six buildings house close to 200 local vendors, but these two are longtime favorites: Wake Robin Farm and Bakery sells artisanal breads, granola, and oat cookies using locally sourced whole wheat from Farmer Ground and white flour from King Arthur. Christiana and Andy Semabia at Better Brittle make West African style peanut and coconut brittle—praised in *Saveur* magazine—and sell fair-trade handwoven baskets. The range of goods available is astonishingly varied; as CNY Regional Market regular Warren Fretwell says, "If you can't find something you are looking for, you aren't looking hard enough." A smaller version runs Thursdays from May through October. Most vendors accept only cash.

2100 Park St., 315-422-8647
cnyregionalmarket.com

Wake Robin Farm
wakerobinfarm.org

Better Brittle
betterbrittle.com

---

### TIP
If you're looking for a specific vendor and somebody tells you, "C shed," knowing the market layout helps. The big covered building closest to the front entrance is A Shed, followed by open-air B Aisle, then C, D, and E Sheds, with the newest at the end: F Shed, which doubles as an event venue.

---

# BRAVE NO-FRILLS BUDA'S
## FOR ROCK-BOTTOM PRICES

This ain't Wegmans and if you're Team Trader Joe's, be warned: you'll either love or hate this deep discount grocery store where boxes may be dinged and some items near their expiration date. Fresh produce and frozen foods can be found up front, packaged goods in back, and in between, a huge walk-in cooler with meats, cheeses, and local Gianelli Sausage on Fridays. Inventory is unpredictable but often includes Starbucks, Stonewall Kitchens, Fever Tree, and Ben & Jerry's. Pepperidge Farm bread is always available for $1.00. There are Italian, Asian, Indian, and Mexican foods, and gluten-free items. You never know what you'll get: fresh flowers, Lee Jeans, even Walmart bras and leggings may turn up, so stock up! Vicki and John will helpfully point out the week's best deals—just ask. And tell them Linda sent you.

Buda's Meats and Produce
2100 Park St., 315-476-0740

---

## TIP
Though Buda's is right next to the Regional Market and shares parking with them, don't go on Saturday—Farmers Market day—it's too crowded. You'll want to take your time to shop and have plenty of room. It's a compact store.

---

# SUPPORT ARTPRENEURS
## OF WILDFLOWERS ARMORY

One customer called it "Etsy in real life," but it's much more than a retail storefront. Wildflowers Armory—"handmade shopping in the heART of downtown"—is a force in the creative community. Jewelry, artwork, body care products, plants, ceramics, clothing, and much more are all handmade by a collective of New York State artisans, many from the Syracuse area. Wildflowers is also an event space hosting warm-weather outdoor Sidewalk Sessions—live local musicians and pop-up vendors every Thursday from May through September. The store name comes from the quote, "Like wildflowers, you must allow yourself to grow in all the places people never thought you would." By nurturing the region's makers, Wildflowers keeps the city's creative spark aglow. So, stop in and feed the fire with your purchase.

217 S. Salina St., 315-546-4919
wildflowersarmory.com

# GO UNDERGROUND
## FOR THE ECLECTIC SHOPS
## OF MCCARTHY MERCANTILE

A dozen storefronts, each distinctive in mood, style, and aesthetic, encircle a common space—a large open area of glass, steel, chrome, and concrete pillars—all in the basement of the terracotta-fronted McCarthy Building, circa 1864. This modern subterranean venue reflects the newest wave of Syracuse retail entrepreneurs backed by the team behind Wildflowers Armory, which has a second smaller shop down here. The Mercantile offers an espresso bar, artisan crafts, thrifted shopping, photography, skateboards, streetwear, vintage decor, candles, T-shirts, art, and accessories. The Mercantile also doubles as a concert space with shows and events year-round. They've hosted the Black Creatives Culture Market, Asian American Pacific Islander Festival, Junk in the Trunk Flea and Vintage Market, and RBC: Rust Belt Craftacular. If it's underground culture, it's underground at the Mercantile.

217½ S. Salina St.
mccarthymercantile.com

---

**TIP**

The only way to access McCarthy Mercantile is through Wildflowers Armory—enter the front door, walk right through and out to the building's indoor atrium, then take the stairs down to the lower level.

---

# REMARK ON THE ROSE-Y SIMILARITIES
## OF H. GREY SUPPLY CO.

City boy moves to the country and opens up a general store with his partner. Sounds like Rose Apothecary from the hit series *Schitt's Creek*, right? It's also the story of H. Grey, a shop more trendy, inclusive, and accessible than the fictional store. Owners Travis Barr—H. Grey's grandson—and Alex Altomonte sell American-made goods, most from small independent New York State businesses. You know those monthly subscription boxes? It's like walking into one. You'll find many delightful items for humans and pets. Travis, a hometown boy whose family owns The Brae Loch Inn down the street, and Alex, from Jacksonville, Florida, met in NYC and moved back here. That explains the urban vibe, but the David Rose similarities? That's the serendipitous fun of H. Grey: sheer coincidence.

53 Albany St., Cazenovia, 315-815-5016

hgreysupplyco.com

# GLOW UP
## AT SYRACUSE FASHION WEEK

As adults, few of us get to play dress-up—unless you're adulting in Central New York. Twice a year, Syracuse Fashion Week challenges local designers to create costumes, hair, makeup, and accessories for three nights of runway shows centered on a theme. Local Love, Farm Fresh Fashion, and Rock Through the Ages inspired past spring shows, while Syracuse Snarl—the October show—goes all-out Halloween: think *Fractured Fairy Tales*, *Living Dolls*, and Hollywood horror films all rolled into one. The Underground Show is SFW's sexiest event; models wear lingerie, body paint, and not much else. These shows—held at hotels, restaurants, and bars—are standing-room-only events, and the final night's posh Gala is at the Landmark Theatre. Each year, ticket sales benefit the Food Bank of CNY.

syracusefashionweek.com

# OOH AND AAH
## AT THE SYRACUSE ARTS AND CRAFTS FESTIVAL

Locals save up their pennies all year to shop this always-packed downtown festival. The annual juried show, which celebrated its 50th year in 2021, brings over 125 artists and fine craftspersons from across the Northeast to Syracuse. Held Friday through Sunday in mid-July, it's a blend of fine arts, graphic arts, photography, woodworking, ceramics, art-to-wear clothing, leatherwork, fiber arts, weaving, metalwork, and sculpture. Buy decorative or functional items, whimsical pieces, or goods suitable for everyday use. According to the Downtown Committee of Syracuse, which organizes the yearly event, it's "recognized as one of the top shows in the country by trade publications." Live music and street performers are part of the free, family-friendly event, and food and beverages are available for purchase.

Cathedral Square
E. Onondaga, E. Jefferson, and Montgomery Sts., 315-422-8284
downtownsyracuse.com

---

### TIP
The vendors on Montgomery Street are local creatives and not part of the juried show, so their price points are often lower than those of artists who've had to travel far to participate. You can find some real bargains here.

# DRIVE OUT FOR THE FARM-FRESH CHARM
## OF 20 EAST

Named after the route it's situated on, this must-visit farm and general store in Cazenovia stocks high-quality goods from local farmers and artisans. Bring a cooler for fresh delectables and packaged grocery items: take them on a picnic at nearby Stone Quarry Hill Art Park or savor them back home. If you don't have a bag, buy one. Their kitchen and homewares—especially the family-run Cazenovia Cut Block items—make perfect host/ hostess gifts, and the local-themed souvenirs are tasteful and elegant. The selection is often surprising: beard oil and lip balm, leather-bound chakra journals, and vintage Native American silver jewelry. Grab some Pastabilities Stretch Bread (delivered every other day) and Hot Tomato Oil if they're not sold out.

85 Albany St., Cazenovia, 315-815-4540
20-east.com

# MEET THE MAKERS
## AT SHOP SMALL SUNDAY

Outside Salt City Market in warmer months (indoors in winter), Shop Small Sunday brings 40-plus vendors together the last Sunday of the month: antiquers, crafters, and creators proud to offer the honest work of their hands and hearts. They can't compete with Amazon—which opened up a Syracuse fulfillment warehouse the same year this once-a-month marketplace was launched—but that's not their goal. They want to look you in the eye, tell you how their products are made, and share the love of what they do. And when you meet your item's maker, that changes what shopping is all about. It's a different energy than clicking through screens; you'll exchange stories, get to know each other, and feel good afterwards. Shop where commerce and community come together in unity.

484 S. Salina St.
saltcitymarket.com/events/shop-small-sunday

# BRING HOME THE LUCK OF THE IRISH
## FROM CASHEL HOUSE

May the road rise up to meet you . . . and lead you to this agent of imported goods from Ireland. Inside this quaint two-story house, Cashel House sells a wide variety of Celtic and Irish items including sterling silver jewelry, claddagh rings, fine woolen goods, Irish Country Pottery, leather accessories, Aran sweaters, Irish pride apparel, hand-carved shamrock boxes, teas and jams, body care and fragrances, and items suitable for birthday, wedding, baby, first Holy Communion, and Confirmation gifts. And then there's the selection of Waterford crystal, including the matching pair of Waterford chandeliers over the register (totaling $3,000) and the three-globe Waterford light fixture by the front door ($1,800) with wine glasses to match. If that's too dear, a lucky lottery scratch-off coin is just five dollars.

224 Tompkins St., 315-472-4438
facebook.com/cashelhousegifts

# BROWSE THE CHARMING BOUTIQUES
## OF HISTORIC CAZENOVIA

Brick and stone construction, arched windows, and cornices give the storefronts along Albany Street an air of distinction. Designated a National Historic District, Cazenovia's commercial downtown dates to the 1800s. Begin at Cazenovia Artisans where pottery, textiles, glass, jewelry, and notecards are showcased in a gallery setting. At Lillie Bean you'll find artful women's and children's apparel and accessories. Cross Albany Street for authentic French goods at Lavender Blue; ten minutes spent among their tablecloths and accessories—imported from Provence and other Mediterranean areas—is like taking a mini trip to France. The Key Consignment Shop has new-to-you upscale clothing and Look Again, a store-within-a-store selling repurposed pieces by students of Cazenovia College's Fashion Design program. *Project Runway* fans, find the next big designer here.

Cazenovia Artisans
39 Albany St., Cazenovia
315-655-2225
cazenoviaartisans.com

Lavender Blue
74 Albany St., Cazenovia
315-655-1095
lavenderblue.bz

Lillie Bean
57 Albany St., Cazenovia
315-655-0677
lilliebean.com

The Key Consignment Shop
66 Albany St., Cazenovia
315-655-3956
thekeyconsign.com

# SHOP A TO Z
## INSIDE MEGA-MALL DESTINY USA

Our mall is so big it has its own zip code. Syracuse's Destiny USA is a six-story juggernaut with four floors of shopping and entertainment. It's New York State's biggest mall—the nation's eighth largest at 2.4 million square feet. Destiny combines retail shopping with outlet stores like Nordstrom Rack, Armani, Coach, Hugo Boss, Kate Spade, Michael Kors, and Brooks Brothers. If your device is your vice, shop the Apple store, Verizon, T-Mobile, AT&T, and Cricket Wireless. Women's clothing is literally covered A to Z from Anthropologie, Athleta, and Ann Taylor to Zumiez; other standouts are Banana Republic, H&M, Lululemon, Macy's, and Urban Outfitters. With over 150 stores, hitting them all is a three-mile route that'll keep you busy on a rainy day.

9090 Destiny USA Dr., 315-466-6000
destinyusa.com

---

## TIP

Right by the main entrance, the Central New York Welcome Center includes the Taste NY Market featuring made-in-New-York products. They stock local food items like artisanal jams, gourmet hot chocolate, maple fudge, and culinary salts. It's a step above last-minute airport shopping, so if you need a Syracuse-themed gift, stop there.

315-436-6341
taste.ny.gov/location/central-new-york-welcome-center

---

# UNEARTH A TREASURE
## AT AMANDA BURY ANTIQUES

This white clapboard house with olive green shutters is a homey place. Especially for the two snow-white terriers—named after characters in *To Kill a Mockingbird*—who rule the roost. There are linens, knick-knacks, jewelry displays, and paintings throughout the downstairs rooms. Upstairs lives the namesake proprietress; she owns the building, so she is able to keep prices reasonable. Approach the cash register and Atticus and Scout will dog your every step, gently barking for treats. Feed them from the dog-shaped candy dish first, then make your purchase. Amanda is a second-generation antique seller who's been doing this for 35 years, so if you want to visit outside store hours, call her: she'll open by appointment. While waiting, peer over the picket fence to glimpse her enchanting backyard garden.

97 Albany St., Cazenovia, 315-655-3326
amandaburyantiques.com

# WHEEL AND DEAL
## AT THE SUNDAY FLEA MARKET

It's equal parts antique show, garage sale, salvage grocery, and surplus inventory sell-off. On Sundays year-round, the Regional Market is where dozens of vendors come to display their wares from 7 a.m. to 2 p.m. "Display" is a loose term. Some sellers meticulously price everything and artfully arrange their goods, while others dump piles of clothing (usually from estate sales) and wait for you to approach, negotiating on the spot. You'll find packaged grocery items, jewelry, home goods, vintage pieces, tools and equipment, furniture, shoes and clothing, the list goes on—both new and previously owned. There are also a handful of coffee and food vendors to keep you fueled and focused on the hunt. Come early for the best deals; on slow days some sellers start packing as early as noon.

2100 Park St., 315-422-8647
cnyregionalmarket.com/flea-market

## TIP

Buy by the armful and you'll get a better price than just holding up one item and saying, "How much?" Listen in on conversations between buyers and sellers. Some vendors like to haggle if you counteroffer. Others shake their heads and say, "I can't go lower—I'm giving you a good deal here." Play it by ear.

# GET INTO THE HOLIDAY SPIRIT
## AT THESE SEASONAL MARKETS

Who says shopping can't be an annual tradition? These three holiday-only events are local favorites because they highlight independent sellers who work hard all year stocking up for eager buyers, many of them repeat customers.

## Junior League of Syracuse Holiday Shoppes

Held in mid-November, this three-day holiday marketplace positions itself as "boutique shopping at its best" and attracts 5,000 shoppers.
Horticulture Bldg. at the NYS Fairgrounds
jlsyracuse.org/holiday-shoppes

## Plowshares Craftsfair and Peace Festival

Central New York's premier multicultural crafts festival is held the first weekend in December. With over 120 craftspeople and community organizations, it's marketed to activists and conscientious consumers with goods centered on compassion, fair trade, and environmental sustainability.
peacecouncil.net/plowshares

## Delavan Studios Open House

A former plow factory converted into an arts warehouse, this three-story complex houses small businesses and artists—painters, graphic designers, woodworkers, sculptors, ceramicists, textile designers—and opens its doors once a year at holiday time.
509 W. Fayette St., 315-800-5032
delavanstudios.com

# SUGGESTED
## ITINERARIES

## SYRACUSE SPECIALTIES

Become a Locavore at the CNY Regional Market, 113

Breakfast 'til You Burst at Mother's Cupboard, 9

Decide the Diner Throw-Down over the Fretta, 16

*Mangia* Old World Specialties in Little Italy, 20

Wolf a Dog or Coney at Heid's, 25

Anticipate While You Wait at Dinosaur Bar-B-Que, 2

Crown the Champ of Chicken Riggies, 5

Polish Off a Polish Feast at Eva's, 24

Risk Brain Freeze at Gannon's Ice Cream, 22

Trade Blarney at Coleman's Authentic Irish Pub, 10

## FUN, FUN, FUN

Immerse Yourself in the Otherworldly Museum of Intrigue, 34

Try Something New at Onondaga County Parks, 76

Learn Why Conservation Matters at the Rosamond Gifford Zoo, 68

Play All Day at the Entertainment Venues of Destiny USA, 61

Score a Home Run of Fun at a Syracuse Mets Game, 66

Step Outside Your Comfort Zone at Canyon Climb Adventure, 67

Harvest Happy Memories at Critz Farms, 49

Putter an Afternoon Away at Fairmount Glen Miniature Golf, 75

• • • • • • • • • • • • • • • • • • • • • • • • • • • •

Break the Ice with Fans at a Syracuse Crunch Game, 73

Get Lit on a Cold Winter's Night at Lights on the Lake, 63

## FREE AND LOW COST ACTIVITIES

Travel Back in Time with the Downtown Historic Walking Tour, 83

Follow Where Mules Once Trod Along the Erie Canal, 54

Stroll Onondaga Lake Park, the "Central Park of CNY," 58

Put Yourself in the Picture with Syracuse Street Art, 104

Flock to the Mall to View Bald Eagles, 62

See Green at the Upside-Down Traffic Light, 81

Go with the Flow along Creekwalk, 102

Harvest Happy Memories at Critz Farms, 49

Hear the Thunder of Cascading Waterfalls, 64

Trace the Underground Railroad through Syracuse's Freedom Trail, 92

Seek Serenity in Upper Onondaga Park, 70

Climb University Hill for Music, Art, and Roses, 94

Swear You're in the Caribbean at Green Lakes, 60

Brave No-Frills Buda's for Rock-Bottom Prices, 114

## BEER/WINE/LIQUOR TRAIL

Trade Blarney at Coleman's Authentic Irish Pub, 10

Harvest Happy Memories at Critz Farms, 49

Raise a Glass to Freedom at Luna Loca, 26

Head to the Hills for Microbrews and Views, 27

Dance to Live Music in an Orchard at Beak & Skiff, 38

• • • • • • • • • • • • • • • • • • • • • • • • • • • •

Toast the Knights of Ni at Middle Ages Brewing, 8

Feel *Wilkommen* at Inclusive Wunderbar, 47

Jam at These Jumpin' Joints for Live Music, 50

## WALKS AND EASY HIKES

Swear You're in the Caribbean at Green Lakes, 60

Rock Around the Lake at Clark Reservation, 74

Stroll Onondaga Lake Park, the "Central Park of CNY," 58

Try Something New at Onondaga County Parks, 76

Bliss Out at Baltimore Woods and Sycamore Hill Gardens, 72

Hear the Thunder of Cascading Waterfalls, 64

Book a Tour or Ghost Walk at Oakwood Cemetery, 96

Wander the Gallery-without-Walls that is Stone Quarry Hill Art Park, 95

Play Out Your Period Drama at Lorenzo State Historic Site, 86

## SYRACUSE LAKEFRONT

Stroll Onondaga Lake Park, the "Central Park of CNY," 58

Practice Gratitude at Skä•noñh, the Great Law of Peace Center, 84

Wolf a Dog or Coney at Heid's, 25

Flock to the Mall to View Bald Eagles, 62

Go with the Flow along Creekwalk, 102

Pump Up the Volume at St. Joe's Amp, 42

● ● ● ● ● ● ● ● ● ● ● ● ● ● ● ● ● ● ● ● ● ● ● ● ● ● ●

# FOODIE EXCURSIONS

Circle Hanover Square for Breakfast, Lunch, and Dinner, 14

Savor Global Goodies at Salt City Market, 3

Cuisine-Hop in Armory Square, 6

Surrender to Flavor at the Cider Mill, 17

Dine Inn Style at a Cazenovia Landmark, 23

Fall for Hot Tom at Pastabilities, 4

Join the Cult-like Fans of Wegmans Grocery Store, 109

# THE ERIE CANAL AND UNDERGROUND RAILROAD

Revisit America's Historic Waterway at the Erie Canal Museum, 85

Walk on (What Once Was) Water at Clinton Square, 57

Travel Back in Time with the Downtown Historic Walking Tour, 83

Become a Syracuse Wise Guy at the OHA, 80

Follow Where Mules Once Trod Along the Erie Canal, 54

Trace the Underground Railroad through Syracuse's Freedom Trail, 92

Raise a Glass to Freedom at Luna Loca, 26

Meet the Mother-in-Law of Oz at the Matilda Joslyn Gage House, 100

# ANTIQUES/HOME DECOR TRAIL

Wheel and Deal at the Sunday Flea Market, 126

Support the ARTpreneurs of Wildflowers Armory, 115

Wax Eloquent on Quarter-Sawn Oak and All Things Stickley, 89

• • • • • • • • • • • • • • • • • • • • • • • • • • •

Take the Stairs at the Syracuse Antique Exchange, 112

Rally 'Round Women-Owned Retail in Marcellus, 110

Unearth a Treasure at Amanda Bury Antiques, 125

Go Underground for the Eclectic Shops of McCarthy Mercantile, 116

Buy Local, Gift Thoughtful at Salt City Artisans, 108

## CONCERT CALENDAR

Be One in a Million at the Great New York State Fair, 30

Choose Your Musical Groove at a Symphoria Concert, 37

Revel in the Dazzle of the Landmark Theatre, 31

Pump Up the Volume at St. Joe's Amp, 42

Strut Your Stuff at the NYS Blues Festival, 40

Dance to Live Music in an Orchard at Beak & Skiff, 38

Jam at These Jumpin' Joints for Live Music, 50

Triple Your Fun at the Oncenter, 36

Climb University Hill for Music, Art, and Roses, 94

Head to the Hills for Microbrews and Views, 27

## CAZENOVIA DAY TRIP

Drive Out for the Farm-Fresh Charm of 20 East, 120

Play Out Your Period Drama at Lorenzo State Historic Site, 86

Browse the Charming Boutiques of Historic Cazenovia, 123

Remark on the Rose-y Similarities of H. Grey Supply Co., 117

Unearth a Treasure at Amanda Bury Antiques, 125

Wander the Gallery-without-Walls That Is Stone Quarry Hill Art Park, 95

Dine Inn Style at a Cazenovia Landmark, 23

• • • • • • • • • • • • • • • • • • • • • • • • • • • •

# LEARN AS YOU GO

Practice Gratitude at Skä•non̄h, the Great Law of Peace Center, 84

Admire American Art at the Everson Museum, 82

Learn Why Conservation Matters at the Rosamond Gifford Zoo, 68

Revisit America's Historic Waterway at the Erie Canal Museum, 85

Feed Your Brain at the MOST, 88

Change Your Mind at Art Galleries Amplifying Diverse Voices, 91

Travel Back in Time with the Downtown Historic Walking Tour, 83

Bliss Out at Baltimore Woods and Sycamore Hill Gardens, 72

Trace the Underground Railroad through Syracuse's Freedom Trail, 92

Baum around Oz-Stravaganza and All Things Oz, 33

Revisit America's Historic Waterway at the Erie Canal Museum, 85

Meet the Mother-in-Law of Oz at the Matilda Joslyn Gage House, 100

# ACTIVITIES
## BY SEASON

## SPRING

Consider Yourself Irish on Green Beer Sunday, 44

Feed Your Brain at the MOST, 88

Stroll Onondaga Lake Park, the "Central Park of CNY," 58

Harvest Happy Memories at Critz Farms, 49

Rock Around the Lake at Clark Reservation, 74

See Green at the Upside-Down Traffic Light, 81

Glow Up at Syracuse Fashion Week, 118

Bliss Out at Baltimore Woods and Sycamore Hill Gardens, 72

Wolf a Dog or Coney at Heid's, 25

Hear the Thunder of Cascading Waterfalls, 64

Wax Eloquent on Quarter-Sawn Oak and All Things Stickley, 89

Go with the Flow along Creekwalk, 102

Meet the Makers at Shop Small Sunday, 121

## SUMMER

Risk Brain Freeze at Gannon's Ice Cream, 22

Play Out Your Period Drama at Lorenzo State Historic Site, 86

Swear You're in the Caribbean at Green Lakes, 60

Pump Up the Volume at St. Joe's Amp, 42

Climb University Hill for Music, Art, and Roses, 94

• • • • • • • • • • • • • • • • • • • • • • • • • • •

Score a Home Run of Fun at a Syracuse Mets Game, 66

Holler at What a Dollar Gets You at Taste of Syracuse, 18

Dance to Live Music in an Orchard at Beak & Skiff, 38

Putter an Afternoon Away at Fairmount Glen Miniature Golf, 75

Ooh and Aah at the Syracuse Arts and Crafts Festival, 119

Fly High at the Jamesville Balloonfest, 41

Strut Your Stuff at the NYS Blues Festival, 40

Rev Up Your Engine at the Syracuse Nationals, 71

Baum around Oz-Stravaganza and All Things Oz, 33

Count Down Summer at Cultural Festivals at Area Churches, 98

Be One in a Million at the Great New York State Fair, 30

## FALL

Pick Apples and More at Beak & Skiff and 1911 Established, 15

Put Yourself in the Picture with Syracuse Street Art, 104

Ask Where They "Get Their Ideas" at the Gifford Author Series, 87

Practice Gratitude at Skä•non̈h, the Great Law of Peace Center, 84

Play All Day at the Entertainment Venues of Destiny USA, 61

Drive Out for the Farm-Fresh Charm of 20 East, 120

Wander the Gallery-without-Walls that is Stone Quarry Hill Art Park, 95

Learn Why Conservation Matters at the Rosamond Gifford Zoo, 68

Keep the Doctor Away at the Lafayette Apple Festival, 32

Choose Your Musical Groove at a Symphoria Concert, 37

Find Your Muse at the YMCA's Downtown Writers Center, 103

Glow Up at Syracuse Fashion Week, 118

Keep It Reel at the Syracuse International Film Festival, 48

• • • • • • • • • • • • • • • • • • • • • • • • • • •

# WINTER

Walk on (What Once Was) Water at Clinton Square, 57

Get Lit on a Cold Winter's Night at Lights on the Lake, 63

Break the Ice with Fans at a Syracuse Crunch Game, 73

Get into the Holiday Spirit at These Seasonal Markets, 128

Flock to the Mall to View Bald Eagles, 62

Eat, Drink and Chill at Winterfest, 43

Applaud the Arts Warmly at Redhouse, 46

Shop A to Z inside Mega-Mall Destiny USA, 124

Bring Home the Luck of the Irish from Cashel House, 122

Try Something New at Onondaga County Parks, 76

Go Underground for the Eclectic Shops of McCarthy Mercantile, 116

Step Outside Your Comfort Zone at Canyon Climb Adventure, 67

Take the Stairs at the Syracuse Antique Exchange, 112

• • • • • • • • • • • • • • • • • • • • • • • • • • •

# INDEX

1911 Established Distillery, 15, 38, 45

20 East, 120, 134, 138

443 Social Club, The, 51

5 Wits, 61

*A Love Letter to Syracuse* Mural, 105

Amanda Bury Antiques, 125, 134

Amazing Mirror Maze, 61

All Things Oz Museum, 33, 135, 138

AnnaBelle Design Company, 110–111

Antique Carousel at Destiny USA, 61

Apex Entertainment, 61

Armory Square, 6–7, 47, 83, 102, 133

Art Galleries, 34, 91, 135

ArtRage, 91

Attilio's, 5

Baghdad Restaurant, 3

Bald Eagles, 62, 131–132, 139

Baltimore Woods Nature Center, 72, 132, 135, 137

Baum, L. Frank, 33, 100–101

Beak & Skiff, 15, 38, 131, 134, 138

Beaver Lake Nature Center, 76–77

Better Brittle, 113

Billy Beez, 61

Biscotti Café and Gelateria, 20

Brae Loch Inn, The, 23, 117

Breadcrumbs Productions, 47

Brewseum, 27

Brew at the Zoo, 69

Brewster Inn, The, 23

Broadway in Syracuse/Famous Artists, 31

Buda's, 114, 131

Butternut Creek Recreation and Nature Area, 55

Byrne Dairy Mint Milk, 45

Café Kubal, 12–13

Camillus Erie Canal Park, 54

Candlelight Series, 7

Canyon Climb Adventure, 67, 130, 139

Carpenter's Brook Fish Hatchery, 76

Cashel House, 122, 139

Cazenovia Artisans, 123

Cazenovia Inns, 23, 133–134

Cedar Bay, 54

Central New York Welcome Center, 124

Chicken Riggies, 4–5, 17, 130

Chittenango Falls State Park, 65

Chittenango Landing Canal Boat Museum, 54

Cider Mill, The, 17, 133

CirqOvation, 37

Civic Center, 36–37

Clark Reservation, 74, 132, 137

*Clinton Serenade* Mural, 105

Clinton Square, 18, 40, 57, 83, 93, 133, 139

CNY Regional Market, 113, 130

Cold Brew Coffee Vodka, 45

Coleman's Authentic Irish Pub, 10, 44, 130–131

Columbus Baking Company, 20

Convention Center, 36

Creekwalk, 102, 131–132, 137

Critz Farms, 49, 130–131, 137

Crouse College, 94

Cultural Festivals at Area Churches, 98–99, 138

Cuse Cycle, 59

Dalton's American Decorative Arts, 89

Delavan Studios Open House, 129

Destiny USA, 34, 61–62, 67, 102, 124, 130, 138–139

Dinosaur Bar-B-Que, 2, 130

Dome, The, 56

YMCA's Downtown Writers Center, The, 103, 138

Eden, 14

E.M. Mills Rose Garden, 94

Enchanted Beaver Lake, 77

Erie Canal Museum, 85, 133, 135

Erie Canal Soaps, 108

Erie Canal State Park, 54

Eva's, 24, 130

Everson Museum, 82, 135

Eyes Graffiti, 104

Fairmount Glen Miniature Golf, 75, 130, 138

Fish Friar, The, 14

Francesca's Cucina, 5

*Freedom Bound* at the OHA, 80

Freedom Trail, 92, 131, 133, 135

Friday Night Porch Party, 38

Friends of the Central Library, 87

Frightmare Farms, 35

Fretta, 16, 130

Funk & Waffles, 51

Gannon's Ice Cream, 22, 99, 130, 137

Gem Diner, 16

George and Rebecca Barnes Foundation, 92

Ghost Walk at Oakwood, 96, 132

Gifford Author Series, 87, 138

Golden Harvest Festival, 77

Green Beer Sunday, 10, 44, 137

Green Hard Cider, 45

Green Lakes Lanes, 5

Green Lakes State Park, 60, 131–132, 137

Gustav Stickley Grave, 97

Gustav Stickley House, 89

Habiba's Ethiopian Kitchen, 21

Hanover Square, 14, 133

Heid's of Liverpool, 25, 130, 132, 137

Heritage Hill Brewhouse, 27

H. Grey Supply Company, 117, 134

Highland Forest, 76

Historic Oakwood Cemetery Preservation Association, 96

Historic Walking Tour of Downtown Syracuse, 83, 131, 133, 135

Honeywell Onondaga Lake Visitor's Center, 62

Hotel Syracuse, 90

Hotel Syracuse Tour, 90

Jamesville Balloonfest, 41, 138

Jamesville Beach Park, 41, 76

Jerry Rescue Monument, 93

Junior League of Syracuse Holiday Shoppes, 129

Jus Sum Jazz, 51

Kasai Ramen, 6

Key Consignment Shop, The, 123

Kitty Hoynes Irish Pub, 6

Kubal Coworks, 21

KultureCity, 34

Lafayette Apple Festival, 32, 138

Lakeview Point Landing, 42

Landmark Theatre, 31, 118, 134

Lavender Blue, 123

Leavenworth Park, 8

Lemon Grass, 6

Liehs & Steigerwald, 20

Lights on the Lake, 63, 131, 139

Lillie Bean, 123

Linklaen House, The, 23

Little Italy, 20–21, 130

Live Music Venues, 8, 27, 32, 38, 41, 44, 46, 50–51, 69, 71, 77, 119, 131–132, 134, 138

Loaded Leprechaun, 45

Local 315 Brewing, 27

Lombardi's Imports, 20

Lorenzo State Historic Site, 86, 132, 134, 137

Luna Loca, 26, 131, 133

Mansion on James, The, 92

Marcellus Mercantile, 110–111

Market Diner, 16

Marriott Syracuse Downtown, 90

Matilda Joslyn Gage House, 100–101, 133, 135

McCarthy Mercantile, 116, 134, 139

Meier's Creek Brewing, 27

Microbreweries, 8, 27, 131, 134

Middle Ages Brewing, 8, 132

Mighty Salt City Mural, 105

Modern Malt, 6

MOST—Museum of Science and Technology, 88, 135, 137

Mother's Cupboard, 9, 130

Mountain Goat Run monument, 70

Museum of Intrigue, The, 34, 130

Music at the Distillery, 38

NBT Bank Stadium, 66

Nestico's, 5

New York State Blues Festival, 40, 134, 138

New York State Fair, 11, 30, 71, 134, 138

Niagara Mohawk (NiMo) Building, 12, 83

Northside, the, 20

Oakwood Cemetery, 96, 132

Old Erie Canal State Park, 54–55, 57

Olive + Fern, 110–111

Oncenter, the, 36, 134

Onondaga County Parks, 76, 130, 131–132, 137, 139

Onondaga Historical Association, 26–27, 80, 83–84, 90, 96

Onondaga Lake Park, 27, 42, 58, 62–63, 131–132, 137

Otro Cinco, 14

Oz-Stravaganza, 33, 135, 138

Pastabilities, 4, 120, 133

Pasta's Daily Bread, 4

Plowshares Craftsfair, 129

Point of Contact/Punto de Contacto Gallery, 91

Pratt's Falls, 65

*Put the U Back in Syracuse* Mural, 105

Redhouse, 46–47, 139

RPM Raceway, 61

Rosamond Gifford Zoo, 68, 130, 135, 138

Rummage Heaven, 110–111

St. Elias Middle Eastern Festival, 99

St. John the Baptist Ukrainian Festival, 99

St. Joseph's Health Amphitheatre, 42

St. Sophia's Greek Fest, 99

Salt City Artisans, 108, 134

Salt City Bar, 3

Salt City Market, 3, 121, 133

Salt Museum, 58

Setnor School of Music, 94

Shifty's, 51

Shop Small Sunday, 121, 137

Shot Clock, 83, 105

Skä●non̈h, the Great Law of Peace Center, 84, 132, 135, 138

Spicy Hot Tomato Oil, 4

Stella's Diner North, 16

• • • • • • • • • • • • • • • • • • • • • • • • • • • • • •

Stickley Furniture Showroom, 89, 97

Stickley Museum, 89

Stone Quarry Hill Art Park, 95, 120, 132, 134, 138

Stone Throwers Park, 81

Summer Concert Series at Beak & Skiff, 38

SU Drama, 39

Sunday Flea Market, 126, 133

Sweet Praxis, The, 14

Symphoria, 37, 134, 138

Syracuse Antique Exchange, 112, 134, 139

Syracuse Arts and Crafts Festival, 119, 138

Syracuse Cooperative Market, 3

Syracuse Crunch, 36, 73, 131, 139

Syracuse Fashion Week, 118, 137–138

Syracuse Freedom Trail, 92, 131, 133, 135

Syracuse International Film Festival, 48, 138

Syracuse Mets, 66, 130, 138

Syracuse Nationals, 71, 138

Syracuse Soapworks, 108

Syracuse Stage, 39

Syracuse Stories, 39

Syracuse Street Art, 104, 131, 138

Syracuse Tree Lighting, 57

Syracuse University, 39, 48, 56, 94, 96

Syracuse University Art Museum, 94

Syracuse University Drama Department, 39

Sycamore Hill Gardens, 72, 132, 135, 137

Taste NY Market, 124

Taste of Syracuse, 18, 138

Thornden Park, 94

Three Falls Woods, 64–65

Tinkers Falls, 64–65

Tipperary Hill, 10, 44, 81

Tree of 40 Fruit, 94

*Trolley* Mural, 105

Underground Railroad, 26, 80, 92, 100, 131, 133, 135

University Hill, 70, 94, 131, 134, 137

Upper Onondaga Park, 70, 131

Upside-Down Traffic Light, 10, 44, 81, 131, 137

Wake Robin Farm and Bakery, 113

War Memorial, 36, 73

Waterfalls, 64–65, 75, 131–132, 137

*We Are the Mighty Salt City Mural,* 105

Wegmans, 55, 109, 114, 133

West Shore Trail, 42, 58, 62

Wildflowers Armory, 115–116, 133

Winterfest, 43, 139

Winter Ice Skating at Clinton Square, 57

*Wizard of Oz*, 33, 100

Women-Owned Retail in Marcellus, 110, 134

WonderWorks, 61, 67

Wren's Den, The, 110–111

Wunderbar, 46–47, 132

*You've Made It . . . & . . . Till Next Time* Mural, 105

Zoo Boo, 69